Advance Praise for *The Soul of the Family Tree*

"In this shrewd memoir, Erickson details how researching her Norwegian-American heritage led to deep personal reflection. The modern ability to investigate one's ancestry using DNA, she argues, can be about more than just biology. Readers may find themselves ordering their own DNA testing kit upon finishing this."

—*Publishers Weekly*

"Lori Erickson traces the 'spiritual DNA' of her Norwegian ancestors, investigating how their heritage influenced their cultural practices and religious beliefs, especially in the midwestern United States. *The Soul of the Family Tree* posits that a spiritual grounding in one's family history can combat 'historical amnesia' and nurture a sense of belonging."

—*Foreword Reviews*

"Can a middle-aged American born in Iowa be a Viking? Yes, if she's as plucky and persistent as Lori Erickson. Starting with her Nordic name, a DNA test, and her strange dislike of *lefse* bread, Erickson takes us on a time-traveling pilgrimage to Newfoundland, Norway, Iceland, and even Istanbul in search of her spiritual DNA. Guided by her Viking foremother Gudrid the Far Traveler, Erickson discovers the well of wisdom by the roots of every family tree—those stories that influence our inner lives—and celebrates the explorer in all of us."

—Nancy Marie Brown, author of *The Far Traveler*
and *The Real Valkyrie*

"*The Soul of the Family Tree* is a terrific new kind of travel book. Lori Erickson takes us on a journey back in time to meet the Vikings, her ancestors (and the ancestors of way too many of us, because, uh, they got around, those Vikings). Enthusiastic, intelligent, and willing to put on a funny Viking skirt and laugh at herself, Lori is the perfect guide for this kind of journey. She asks the questions we would be asking, and then she

trots off to the next destination filled with boundless energy. This truly entertaining book should be on the shelf of everyone who is interested in family history, genealogy, or who has ever wondered, 'Where do I come from, really?'"
—June Melby, author of *My Family and Other Hazards*

"Lori Erickson has not only the adventurous spirit of her Viking ancestors but a sparkling sense of humor not generally associated with Olaf the Stout or Ivar the Boneless. Deftly navigating the promises and perils of DNA testing, ancient sagas, family lore, historical reenactments, homelands, hometowns, and stupid graffiti left behind by your ancestors, *The Soul of the Family Tree* takes us on a journey into human identity that's both fun and profound."
—Scott Samuelson, author of *The Deepest Human Life* and *Seven Ways of Looking at Pointless Suffering*

"Despite her dig at Swedes, Lori Erickson has put together a must-read for all fans of genealogy. Her journey is one that will inspire everyone to dig in and experience the power of knowing their ancestral roots."
—Brian Gerard, pastor and winner of Swedish-American reality show *Allt för Sverige*, season 1

"Captivating . . . I literally could not put this one down! Not only did I learn a great deal, but I found the book to be very fascinating and entertaining. While I am not personally of Scandinavian descent, I now want to visit important places described in the book and start researching the stories of my own ancestors. Highly recommended!"
—Brian Allain, founder of Writing for Your Life and curator of *How to Heal Our Divides*

The Soul of the Family Tree

Also by Lori Erickson

Near the Exit: Travels with the Not-So-Grim Reaper
Holy Rover: Journeys in Search of Mystery, Miracles, and God

The Soul of the Family Tree

Ancestors, Stories, and the Spirits We Inherit

Lori Erickson

WJK WESTMINSTER
JOHN KNOX PRESS
LOUISVILLE · KENTUCKY

First Edition
Published by Westminster John Knox Press
Louisville, Kentucky

21 22 23 24 25 26 27 28 29 30—10 9 8 7 6 5 4 3 2 1

Map and illustration on page 10 by Claudia McGehee.

Illustration on page 84 by Charles Edward Brock, *The Heroes of Asgard: Tales from Scandinavian Mythology* (London: Macmillan, 1930), 36.

Book design by Drew Stevens
Cover design by designpointinc.com

Library of Congress Cataloging-in-Publication Data is on file at the Library of Congress, Washington, DC.

ISBN-13: 978-0-664-26703-2

PRINTED IN THE UNITED STATES OF AMERICA

♾ The paper used in this publication meets the minimum requirements of the American National Standard for Information Sciences—Permanence of Paper for Printed Library Materials, ANSI Z39.48-1992

For my ancestors,
including Gudrid, Leif, Hans, and Sila

GREENLAND

Brattahlid

Atlantic Ocean

CANADA

L'Anse aux Meadows

NEWFOUNDLAND

TO AMERICA

VIKING ROUTES
in the 9th-11th Centuries

LMK

Contents

On the west coast of Iceland, a statue honors the Norse explorer Gudrid the Far Traveler. (PHOTO BY ECHO IMAGES / ALAMY STOCK PHOTO)

Prologue
A Genealogical Golden Ticket

I'm wandering through what was once one of the greatest churches in Christendom: Hagia Sophia in Istanbul. As a guide and I walk through its aged, echoing grandeur, he helps me imagine what it must have looked like to worshipers when it was completed in the year 537. Topped by a dome that seemed to float in the air as if suspended on strings from the heavens, its interior glittered with mosaics, icons, holy relics, and colored marble, all lit by thousands of flickering candles and lamps.

"This church was so grand, so opulent and huge, that many worshipers could hardly believe what they were seeing," the guide says. "They didn't know if they were on earth or in heaven."

Climbing to its second-floor gallery, we find a vantage point overlooking the expanse below, a space now filled with hundreds of chattering tourists. The guide continues his story, explaining that Hagia Sophia—meaning "Holy Wisdom" in Greek—was built using materials brought from throughout the Byzantine Empire. For a thousand years it stood as the world's largest cathedral, the crown jewel of a city known at the time as

Constantinople, named in honor of Constantine, the emperor who made Christianity the dominant religion in the Roman Empire. After the city became part of the Ottoman Empire in 1453, Hagia Sophia became a mosque, and to this day it shows an intertwining of the two spiritual traditions.

The guide then points to some marks on a marble parapet, etched lines that look like chicken scratches. "This graffiti was left by a Viking, probably in the ninth century," he says. "It means something like 'Halvdan was here.'"

I look in surprise at the marks, which I can now see are indeed Norse runes. The Vikings were here, in Constantinople? I had a flash of a tall, bearded, muscular man, a native of the pagan Northland, looking down at an elaborate liturgy on the main floor of the church. He watches as ornately dressed priests and acolytes walk in formation to the altar, chanting and singing, wreathed in clouds of incense. Then, with a grunt, the bored Viking takes out a knife and carves his name into the marble.

Honestly. What kind of person scratches his name into a church balcony, especially in this cathedral, the most beautiful in the Christian world? And then I realize I know exactly who would do such a thing—my people.

You might notice my last name is Scandinavian: Erickson, the son of Erick. For much of my adult life I considered it a relatively minor part of my identity. I was just one of a multitude of Americans whose ancestors hailed from a part of the world associated with skiing, pickled herring, and bleak Nordic noir crime dramas that belie the region's reputation as one of the happiest places in the world. But sometime in my mid-fifties, it was as if a switch flipped on, and discovering more about my ancestors became a passion. I'd latched onto genealogy, the quintessential hobby of middle age.

As we grow older and more relatives start to disappear from the family lifeboat, many of us develop a new interest in those who've slipped overboard. People tend to stake out a particular focus in their genealogical searches. Some trace the medical histories of their ancestors, looking for genetically linked diseases to explain their health deficits or give them a heads-up on what to worry about. Those wanting to join the Daughters of the American Revolution search for ancestors who aided in the fight for independence; others do research to try to verify a family story about kin who walked the Cherokee Trail of Tears. Adoptees seek clues to their biological relatives while some search for famous distant cousins, from Queen Elizabeth and Abraham Lincoln to Oprah and Dolly Parton. Members of the Church of Jesus Christ of Latter-day Saints do genealogy as a religious obligation, wanting to give everyone, even the dead, the chance to become part of their faith. Others try to connect with distant cousins alive today, tracking down relatives in the places where their ancestors once lived. Each of us has a unique motivation for finding our way through the ever-proliferating thicket of facts, dates, birth certificates, death notices, immigration records, and census data, made more accessible than ever before by the Internet.

At first it was the mapping of my family tree that intrigued me the most. I gathered bits and pieces of records, traipsed through cemeteries to hunt for grave markers with familiar names, searched online to connect with other family trees (thank you, second cousin once removed, for doing research that I have happily appropriated as my own). At one point I remember leaning back in my desk chair with satisfaction, looking at the chart that filled the computer monitor in front of me. The names and dates extended back five generations, dozens of relatives who came together in a precise combination just so that I could be born. I looked at my name, there in a box at the very bottom, and felt grateful when I realized that all of human history (or at least a section of it that had settled in northern Europe) had conspired to produce the precise genetic combination that led to Glorious Me. Even one alternative choice, one great-grandmother who'd married the elder brother and not the younger one, and I'd be slightly different. But no, instead they all came together to fulfill my destiny.

Then, with a sigh, I admitted the ridiculousness of this thought, especially after I added my two sons to my genealogy chart, spoiling the beautiful symmetry of all those boxes culminating in my name. I realized that they, too, could view themselves as the climax of human history. And I had the unsettling thought that at some point in the future I'd be just another ancestor to my descendants, a small box with birth and death dates, and maybe a link to a census record.

But as interest in my own genetic heritage faded somewhat, a larger fascination blossomed. I became increasingly intrigued by the ways in which I'm the product of forces emanating from deep in the past and lands far away. I realized that some of the traits I thought were mine alone were actually passed down to me, and that I shared much more with my ancestors than just some strands of DNA. I learned about Viking history, seeking connections between my perpetual wanderlust and the seafaring exploits of my distant forebears. Books on modern Scandinavia gave me insights into the cultural patterns that have been passed down through generations in my family, from why spices were considered suspicious substances in my mother's kitchen to why many of the men in my family hoard their words like they have to pay for them by the syllable.

I began to see, too, how the spiritual history of my family mirrored larger trends. The Vikings who once worshiped Thor and Odin converted to Christianity around the year 1000, eventually becoming not just Lutheran, but Über-Lutheran. Today, however, just a small percentage of Scandinavians attend church regularly, a reflection of a secular wave that washed across Western Europe after World War II and is now lapping at the shores of America. How did my family's history reflect this shift? And how did my personal spiritual journey fit into this larger story?

In my explorations, I've learned that what I'm really searching for is my spiritual DNA. There's not a test I can take to identify this mix, no spitting into a test tube to find my religious genealogy. But the process of learning about my heritage has taught me a great deal about the swirling patterns of my inner life, and I've come to see the ways my story reflects something larger, a shift from a pagan world to a Christian one and then to a secular culture that nonetheless longs for transcendence.

Genealogy is one of the world's most popular hobbies. Thanks to the Internet and DNA analysis, it's never been easier to trace your family tree and tie it into an ever-expanding web of genealogical records. Once people begin to research this information, many set out to connect with physical traces of their family's past as well. They usually don't focus on the places highlighted in guidebooks—the grand palaces and sites of famous battles—but instead on the homely landmarks of ordinary lives: a farm in Ireland once tilled by a grandfather; the Japanese village that a great-grandmother left as a young woman, journeying to meet a man in San Francisco she knew only from a photograph; a parish record of baptisms and marriages in a Sicilian church; a graveyard in the Ukraine; or a plantation in Alabama where slaves once toiled. Because of curiosity about genealogy, these places of little interest to the larger world get remembered and honored.

As a writer with a lifelong interest in the intertwining of spirituality and travel, it's clear to me that many of these trips are actually pilgrimages—life-changing journeys that relate to questions of identity and meaning. People go searching for information about their ancestors but come home having discovered just as much about themselves. And even though we may not be Sicilian, or Japanese, or Ukrainian, the stories of their journeys often touch something deep within us as well. It's why Alex Haley's *Roots: The Saga of an American Family* became a bestseller in the 1970s and why TV series like *Genealogy Roadshow* and *Finding Your Roots* attract millions of viewers. In hearing other people's stories, we see reflections of our own inner journeys.

My research on my family tree has made me realize that rather than a mere list of names and dates, genealogy can be an invitation to imagine, to ponder, and to learn not just who our ancestors were but who we are and who we might become. I think of it as a golden ticket that gives me permission to explore obscure corners of history, meet remarkable characters, and trace my spiritual DNA, the soul material that makes me who I am.

I hope my example will send you on your own genealogical and spiritual quest. You might find that your soul has been shaped by your ancestors and that they continue to influence you. I know my climb up my family tree has affected my spiritual life in unexpected ways, including igniting a fascination for Norse mythology and metaphysics. In making these myths my own, I've gained access to a deep well of wisdom that I never would have discovered if I hadn't started poking around in my ancestral attic.

Whatever your ancestry, you may have more connections to the peoples of the North than you realized. If you get your DNA tested, some Scandinavian might show up in your results, even if the rest of your ancestors came from lands far away. The Norse influence also threads through our language and culture. Perhaps you're reading this on a Tuesday (named after the Norse god Tyr), Wednesday (named after Wodan, the Old Saxon form of Odin), Thursday (Thor's day), or Friday (which honors Odin's wife, Frigg). If you've ever played Dungeons and Dragons, watched *Game of Thrones*, or read one of the thousands of fantasy books influenced by Tolkien's *The Lord of the Rings*, you've been entertained by Norse myths. Or check your phone: its Bluetooth function is named after Harald Bluetooth, a tenth-century Viking king (the ᛒ symbol blends the first letters of his name written in runes).

I've come to believe that the Norse have something to teach all of us at a deeper level as well. I think their larger-than-life story speaks to something universal in the human psyche, reminding us that we need adventure and risk and that our spirits wither when we stay cocooned in our twenty-first-century equivalent of isolated villages, relating to the world mainly through digital screens.

My search for ancestors took me from the bleak coast of Newfoundland and the stunning fjords of Norway to the deck of a modern-day Viking ship. I paid my respects to a Norse saint with highly suspect credentials and knelt to gather dirt from the tiny plot of land my great-great-grandfather once farmed. I came to a new understanding of the Norwegian-American small town where I grew up, and I traveled to another corner of the Midwest where I learned that even a hoax can reveal truths about the past. I visited dead Vikings in the north of England, met modern-day Norse pagans in Minneapolis, and spent a weekend pretending to be a Viking woman at a reenactor festival. And I realized that I'm never going to like the flatbread *lefse*, no matter how many times I try that Norwegian-American staple.

My quest makes me think of the "Cosmic Eye" video that periodically gets passed around on Facebook, the one that begins by showing a young woman lying on a patch of grass. The camera starts to move upward, zooming ever farther into space, past the moon, past our solar system, through the Milky Way and into the farthest reaches of the galaxy. Then the journey reverses, telescoping back to earth once again; only this time the camera heads into the body of the woman, going through her skin to enter her organs and ever deeper into her cells and molecules and then down to the atomic level, which has an uncanny resemblance to outer space. Both of those journeys spin out from a young woman lying on the grass, just as each of us is poised between the past and the future, between our ancestors and our descendants, and between a too-often unexplored inner world and a dazzlingly complex outer world.

Once you start doing genealogy, you realize how many worlds are connected to you.

The idea for this book began with a bathroom break, which just goes to show that you never know when inspiration will strike. My husband, Bob, and I were traveling by car on the Ring Road of Iceland, winding our way across a landscape of jagged mountains, bleak plains, vast glaciers, and slumbering volcanoes. Driving across the Snæfellsnes Peninsula one misty, cool morning, I told Bob I needed to make a stop.

A few miles down the road, he pulled into a roadside park. Looking in vain for a restroom, I made use of the lee side of a

rock, which in Iceland is often as good as you get while traveling. After taking care of my business, I looked with interest at
a statue that stood nearby. It showed a strong and confident-
looking woman standing on top of a stylized representation of
a Viking longboat. On her shoulder perched a child, whom she
steadied with one hand as she looked off into the distance with
a determined gaze. The adjacent sign identified the woman as
Gudrid the Far Traveler. The name seemed appropriate, given
the map that detailed her journeys. Lines led from Iceland
to Greenland and then to the New World, while another set
traced a route from Iceland to Norway and Denmark, and then
to Rome and back.

Intrigued, I read the text below the map. Gudrid, whose
story is told in the Icelandic sagas, was a sister-in-law of the
famous explorer Leif Eriksson. She gave birth to the first child
of European descent in the New World, living there for several years in the early eleventh century before the colony failed.
After she returned to Iceland, she became a nun and later sailed
to Denmark and walked to Rome on pilgrimage. Eventually she
came home to Iceland, where she lived out her days renowned
for her courage, wisdom, and kindness. She was likely the most
well-traveled woman of the Middle Ages.

I got back in the car and turned to Bob. "That was a good
stop," I told him. "I think I just found my foremother."

ILLUSTRATION BY CLAUDIA McGEHEE

1

DNA: The Lazy Person's
Entry into Genealogy

Early one morning, before I'd had even a sip of my morning coffee, I started collecting my spit. I'd never thought much about salivating before—it was something my mouth did without being told—and making it a voluntary process was surprisingly difficult. I thought about cows chewing their cud, then tried to imagine eating ice cream. Ever so slowly, the liquid accumulated around my teeth and under my tongue, finally giving me enough to spit into a small tube. I repeated the process, this time imagining snacking on a cupcake.

My goal was to fill a small, plastic vial sent to me from a company based in Lehi, Utah. If I gave some strangers there enough saliva, they promised to unlock the secrets of my DNA. As I held the filled-at-last container up to the light, I saw a layer of bubbles topping the viscous fluid like a foamy head on a glass of Guinness. I marveled at what this fluid contained: information about my genetic blueprint and also help in digesting whatever I put into my mouth, from Thai peppers to bean soup. It was an amazingly versatile liquid.

I sealed the tube and packed it into a prepaid box. As I dropped it into a mailbox on my morning walk, I thought about the technicians who spend their days unpacking saliva sent to them from around North America. AncestryDNA, the company that was about to receive my package, has processed the tests of more than fifteen million people. I resisted the urge to calculate just how many barrels of spit that entailed.

Several weeks later, I got the results. Through a mysterious scientific process that I didn't even attempt to understand, my saliva, bubbles and all, had revealed the following recipe for Lori Erickson:

— 81 percent Norwegian
— 16 percent Swedish
— 3 percent from Ireland and Scotland

It showed that family lore was correct: I am among the least ethnically diverse citizens in America. I tried to take comfort in the smidgeon of Celtic DNA in my mix. It explains my passion for Irish music, men in kilts, and the poetry of William Butler Yeats, I thought, plus the way my ears perk up whenever I hear a Scottish brogue. The Swedish part was a bit disappointing, however, given the fact that I'd been raised to believe that Norwegians are the best type of Scandinavians, the most industrious and friendly, while the Swedes are—well, Swedes. No one had ever revealed to me that our family line was tainted by them.

In some ways, doing genealogy in this way felt like cheating. Instead of straining to read grainy microfilm records in a small-town library or traipsing across rural graveyards, all I needed to do was click through the links provided in an e-mail. As if by magic, page after page of information was revealed. First came a map showing the areas where my ancestors likely lived, with two circles centered in different regions in Norway and another encompassing Ireland and Scotland. Another link gave information on Norwegian immigration, telling how millions of people came to the United States during the nineteenth century because of poverty and a lack of economic opportunities in their native country. The promise of cheap land lured many to the upper Midwest (I mentally added "including to my hometown of Decorah, Iowa, perhaps the most Norwegian-American community in existence"). There they broke the prairie with plows, endured the winters, and no doubt sorely missed the magnificent mountains and fjords of their home-land as they looked out across the gently rolling landscape of the Great Plains.

Another click led to a list of 620 potential relatives, who were grouped into possible second, third, and fourth cousins. I recognized some of the names in the second-cousin category, but none in the third- and fourth- ones. Choosing a distant cousin at random, with a few more clicks I revealed our common ancestors, my great-great-grandparents. I savored the formidable Norwegianness of their names: Hans Ørbech Henrikssøn Bjørager and Sila Bårdsdatter Halverson. Both were born in Lærdal, Sogn og Fjordane, Norway; Hans, in 1815, and Sila, in 1827. Hans had traveled on a ship from Bergen to the United States in the summer of 1850, arriving in New York on July 15, 1850. On October 27 of that same year he married Sila (no record of when she crossed the ocean, and I wondered if they'd known each other in Norway or just had a speedy courtship). Hans died in Decorah in 1890; Sila in 1904.

It was as if I'd received a letter from a stranger who mysteri-ously knew a myriad of details about my personal life. All from a little tube of saliva.

DNA DETECTIVE WORK

The fact that millions of people have traced their ancestry through DNA analysis is something entirely new in human history, the combination of scientific know-how and a dra-matic lowering of the price. For less than $100 and a DNA sample (typically collected from either saliva or a cheek swab), we can get a peek into our ancestral past and the inner work-ings of our genes.

Genetic genealogy, as it's often called, usually involves three types of tests, each named after which part of the genetic material is analyzed:

— Y-chromosomal testing is done only on men, because they're the ones who carry the Y chromosome. While the results are typically done to trace male lineage, women can ask a close male relative to take the test to gain information about their ancestry.

— Mitochondrial DNA testing can be done on anyone, though it traces genetic material inherited only through the maternal lineage (mitochondrial DNA is passed from a mother to her children).

— Autosomal testing looks at the twenty-two pairs of chromosomes shared by both males and females. In addition to giving information on ethnicity, it can be used to determine paternity or trace genetically linked medical conditions.

Now, if you're worried that this book is going to wander too far into the scientific weeds, be assured that the genetics lesson isn't going to last long, and waiting in the wings are characters who include Leif the Lucky, Olaf the Stout, and Ivar the Boneless, plus an ax-murdering Viking woman. Fossilized Viking poop will make a cameo appearance, and I'll explain why the Web of Wyrd might help explain the weirdness in your family. So bear with me on the science lesson, which is a necessary foundation for anyone doing genealogy in the modern age.

As I read about genetic genealogy, even with my limited scientific background I could appreciate the complexities and controversy that surround the tests, especially the inexpensive kits that come in the mail. It turns out that the percentages in my Lori Erickson recipe are not as precise as I'd thought (and they can't actually explain my love for Irish music or fondness for a Scottish brogue). I took an autosomal test, but if I'd sent my spit to other companies, I'd likely not get the exact same set of results, though hopefully there'd be considerable overlap. In other words, such tests deal in approximations and probabilities, though the companies say that their accuracy will improve as more people get tested and their databases grow.

If you're contemplating spitting into a vial, you should also think hard about what you want to have revealed. Some tests can reveal medical information—again, in probabilities rather than certainties, but enough to keep you awake at night if you're a worrier. I knew I didn't want to receive a heads-up that I might be susceptible to conditions like Parkinson's or Alzheimer's. If there's a sword hanging over my head, I don't want to know about it until it actually falls.

Privacy advocates raise other concerns about DNA testing, pointing out the potential problems of handing your genetic data to a third party. If you've seen enough sci-fi movies, you know what can happen if this information falls into the wrong hands (and even today, this information has been used to crack criminal cases, raising questions about just how private the data is). Corporations have safeguards to shield the identities of those being tested, but reading the fine print in their privacy policies is a good idea.

The testing company I used gave me the additional option of downloading my raw DNA data, an option that amazed me. For millennia, no one, not even the wealthiest and most powerful, had access to this information—in fact, they didn't even know such information existed. But today, thanks to the labors of thousands of scientists (as well as engineers who figured out a way to process the tests cheaply), the information is made available to anyone with one hundred dollars to spare.

After I downloaded the data, I started reading:

rs1902147231693625TT
rs31319721752721AG
rs125620341768448AG
rs1150939051787173GG
rs66810491800007CC

rs284446991830181AA

rs49703831838555CC

rs49703821840753TT

rs115161851843405AA

rs44756911846808CC

Trust me—it doesn't get any more interesting than this. The results go on and on and on, revealing thousands of numbers and letters that provide the basis for my biological existence. They explain my hair color and my height, how my ears are shaped, and the fact that I write with my right hand. What would've been the result if the A and G had gotten switched on the third row? I'd never know, but once again I had the sense of mysterious forces coming together to make me who I am.

The long chain of numbers and letters made it possible for AncestryDNA to make an estimate of my ethnic mix. I initially thought they'd compare my results to the DNA of Norwegians from the mid-nineteenth century, during the period when Hans and Sila immigrated (I imagined white-coated scientists sampling corpses in rural Norway, a picturesque fjord in the background). Instead, technicians compared my information to a database of results from living people in more than a thousand regions around the world. Because much of my DNA is similar to that of Norwegians alive today, it's probable that we share common ancestors. No tissue from dead Scandinavians was needed after all.

Researchers have used DNA technology to peer much farther back in time. They've even identified a woman known as Mitochondrial Eve, who lived about 150,000 years ago, and Y-Chromosomal Adam, who walked the earth at approximately the same time (give or take thousands of years). Geneticists have traced the Y-chromosomes and mitochondrial DNA of contemporary humans to these two people, both of whom lived in Africa. The fact that they never met, let alone mated, doesn't make any difference. They're our genetic mother and father.

While creationists aren't convinced by this research, still believing in a literal Adam and Eve who lived together in the garden of Eden, the science nicely supports a fundamental premise of many faiths: we're all related. Because all humans trace their ancestry to Mitochondrial Eve and Y-Chromosomal Adam, everyone who's ever lived, as well as everyone alive today, could be invited to your family reunion. In fact, we share 99.9 percent of our DNA with other *Homo sapiens* and a surprisingly large percentage with the nonhuman world. With chimpanzees, it's 98 percent; with mice, it's 97 percent. And what about the fruit flies flitting around the compost bin in your garden? They're kin, too, because about 44 percent of our DNA is similar. Especially in an age with so many divisions, it's refreshing to be reminded that what we share is so much greater than what separates us.

DNA testing can solve family mysteries, stir up controversy, and contradict cherished family stories. People who proudly claim to be Irish have found only a wee drop in their genes. White supremacists have discovered they have African ancestry. Adoptees have connected with long-lost relatives while others have learned they're not genetically related to any of their siblings.

Canine DNA testing is also a booming business, though it never leads to any angst on the part of the dog. No poodle has ever been devastated when it was revealed that it carries basset hound genes. And even when the analysis is used to determine which dog owners are neglecting to pick up poop in upscale communities, the pup remains unfazed.

Within my circle of friends, DNA testing is all the rage. Dick, a German-Irish-English native of Des Moines, discovered that he has some Nigerian DNA. Milwaukee-born Brian learned that he has Polynesian DNA in his mix. Ellen, who'd hoped for a link to Asia, was disappointed to have to settle for a potpourri of northern European ethnicity. Helen thought that she was Italian but has to be content with being mostly German.

I'm struck by the conversations about family lore that unfold, revealing aspects of my friends' lives that I didn't know.

It turns out that Scott, who grew up in small-town Iowa, had great-grandparents who were born in Lebanon. Mary is related to both Che Guevara and Ulysses S. Grant ("I'm from warrior stock way back," she says). Tom is descended from someone who saved Henry VIII from drowning, a good deed that netted him a knighthood. And Jennifer grew up with stories about being descended from samurai nobility in Japan. I can't help but look at them a little differently after learning about the ancestors standing behind them.

I was struck by a comment made by my friend Rebecca. "I'd always thought I was English," she said. "But then I had my DNA tested and realized I have just as much Irish in my background. It changed how I thought about myself. I'm the same person as I was before, and yet I'm not."

I'm surprised, too, by how often Scandinavia appears in people's DNA results. The region, after all, is in an isolated and remote part of Europe, the equivalent to North Dakota in the United States. People who live in California can go for years, even entire lifetimes, without meeting a North Dakotan. But Scandinavia pops up in people's DNA results again and again. A friend-of-a-friend from Ghana, for example, was surprised to discover Scandinavian DNA in her mix, although as far as she knows, her family line is rooted solely in Africa.

"It's the Vikings," I told people who were surprised to learn they've some Norse in their genes. "Back before the Scandinavians got civilized, they raided Europe." People nodded, satisfied with the explanation. But I found myself increasingly intrigued by how often my ancestors had traveled by longboat into other people's ancestral gene pools.

With DNA results in hand, I started inputting information into genealogical software, using bits and pieces of data scavenged from family Bibles and learned from relatives. One by one I added names to my family tree, recording the dates of their births, marriages, and deaths. I had a great deal of information for three generations, but after that the details got sparser. It helped that the software program provided me with hints, suggesting additional names and inviting me to review documentation such as census records and grave markers.

I was surprised by the amount of data available for free on the Internet, much of it digitized by volunteers wanting to help other genealogists. A veritable army of ancestor-obsessed people spend their spare time recording the information on headstones, transcribing the spidery writing of old ledgers, and uploading photos to the wonderfully named DeadFred.com, a genealogy photo archive. Seeing the cascade of personal details on websites made me realize that anyone with a keen sense of personal privacy shouldn't take up genealogy as a hobby.

My own web spread ever wider. I found my first ancestor who lived during the eighteenth century: Anne Oldsdatter Hegg (the mother of my great-great-grandfather Hans), who was born January 1, 1787, in Lærdal, Sogn og Fjordane, Norway. I wondered if her parents were happy about having a New Year's baby—a thought that made me feel an unmistakable tug of a connection to those long-dead relatives.

Let me now heap lavish praise upon the Church of Jesus Christ of Latter-day Saints, echoing nearly every book on genealogy written within the past fifty years. That's because its members have revolutionized—and democratized—genealogy. Thanks to their generosity, people can amass a huge amount of information on relatives without ever bothering to get up from their computers. In the process, genealogy research has become much easier for everyone.

Genealogy is important to members of the Utah-based church because they believe that people need to be baptized into their faith if they're going to live eternally. This poses a problem for those who died before the church came into existence in 1830. The solution is baptism-by-proxy, a rite performed in Latter-day Saints temples. This gives the departed the choice to either accept or reject the faith. People are encouraged to trace their ancestry to ensure that their extended family stays together for eternity.

This practice gained attention and generated a considerable amount of controversy when it became known in the mid-1990s that members had baptized by proxy Jews who died during the Holocaust. It was done with good intentions, but many Jews, not surprisingly, found it offensive. Church officials formally apologized, removed the Jewish names from their archives, and promised to discontinue the practice. Despite this response by the church hierarchy, Jewish names have still been found in the records, but they've been added by individuals acting on their own and are removed whenever they're discovered.

This zeal for tracking down ancestors wouldn't mean much to genealogy buffs if it weren't for the church's generosity in sharing its information. The Family History Library in Salt Lake City is the world's largest repository of genealogical records. Its collection contains more than 1.4 million rolls of microfilm and 600,000 books, serials, and maps. Staff members and volunteers help visitors find books and records, analyze what they uncover, identify their next research steps, decipher old-fashioned handwriting, and translate non-English documents. For those who can't make a pilgrimage to Salt Lake City, the library is connected to a network of family history centers all over the world, staffed by volunteers who help people trace their roots. Millions more records are made available online each year.

I visited the central Family History Library a decade ago, back when my interest in tracing my ancestry was no more than idle curiosity. The building is part of Temple Square in downtown Salt Lake City, the headquarters for the Church of Jesus Christ of Latter-day Saints. I watched a brief orientation video and then was matched with a woman who became my personal guide, sitting next to me at a computer as she taught me the basics of searching records. Within a few minutes she helped me find pages from the 1930 census that showed information on my father and grandfather. Seeing their names written in cursive on a ledger page was surprisingly moving, bringing to mind the clerk who'd laboriously recorded the names of farm families during the Great Depression. During the next hour

I hop-skipped my way through other websites that gave me more information on previous generations, including the name of the town in Norway from which my grandfather's parents had immigrated: Hadeland. I looked it up on a map and day-dreamed about making a trip to Norway someday.

But when I got home, I tucked the information away in a file and forgot about it, because the genealogy bug hadn't bitten me yet.

CHRONICLING THE BEGATS

The Church of Jesus Christ of Latter-day Saints, more than any other religious group, has an appreciation for the intertwining of spirituality and family history. But genealogy also has deep roots in the larger Judeo-Christian tradition. Consider the beginning of the book of 1 Chronicles, which details who begat whom through the centuries:

> Adam, Seth, Enosh; Kenan, Mahalalel, Jared; Enoch, Methuselah, Lamech; Noah, Shem, Ham, and Japheth.
>
> The descendants of Japheth: Gomer, Magog, Madai, Javan, Tubal, Meshech, and Tiras. . . . The descendants of Ham: Cush, Egypt, Put, and Canaan. The descendants of Cush: Seba, Havilah, Sabta, Raama, and Sabteca. The descendants of Raamah: Sheba and Dedan. Cush became the father of Nimrod; he was the first to be a mighty one on the earth.
>
> (1 Chron. 1:1–5, 8–10)

The begats go on and on, a perfect distillation of why many people think genealogy is mind-numbingly dull. The endless lists of names. The lack of context, detail, and story. The assumption that we should care about people just because they happened to be related to someone important. The begats have a musty, moldy smell about them, sniffable even from the distance of millennia. They're the equivalent of the cousin who corners you at a family reunion to show you a three-ring binder filled with information on relatives you've never met, never will meet, and never want to meet.

And I wager that no one in history has asked to have these verses read to them for comfort. No dying mother ever says, "Son, after you finish the Twenty-third Psalm, could you read that list of names from First Chronicles? Start with the Sons of Cush. They're my favorites."

In the Gospels, the book of Matthew has its own version of the begats, a set of verses that trace the lineage of Jesus all the way back to Adam (not the Y-chromosomal one but the guy living in the garden of Eden). I won't quote the entire list, just the part that starts with King David:

> David was the father of Solomon by the wife of Uriah, and Solomon the father of Rehoboam, and Rehoboam the father of Abijah, and Abijah the father of Asaph, and Asaph the father of Jehoshaphat, and Jehoshaphat the father of Joram, and Joram the father of Uzziah, and Uzziah the father of Jotham, and Jotham the father of Ahaz, and Ahaz the father of Hezekiah, and Hezekiah the father of Manasseh, and Manasseh the father of Amos, and Amos the father of Josiah, . . . and Eliud the father of Eleazar, and Eleazar the father of Matthan, and Matthan the father of Jacob, and Jacob the father of Joseph the husband of Mary, of whom Jesus was born, who is called the Messiah.
>
> (Matt. 1:6–10, 15–16)

What's so wonderfully peculiar about this is that according to the Gospels, Joseph wasn't the biological father of Jesus— God was. This is the highest profile instance of what genealogists call a "nonpaternity event," meaning that the biological dad isn't the same as the one publicly acknowledged. It's happened with great frequency in history—since a culture's sexual morality is often honored in theory more than in reality—but it's still amusing to see this enshrined in the Bible.

Genealogy has been of interest to many other cultures as well. Ancient civilizations often had rulers who claimed descent from gods, and the nobility of all eras typically kept elaborate family trees, like ranchers maintaining precise breeding records for their cattle. In Europe, especially, the wealthy and powerful used genealogy to prove their elite status and keep the riffraff out of the family gene pool (though the descendants of Queen Victoria could have benefited from new breeding stock, given their propensity to the genetically linked disease of hemophilia).

Venturing further afield, genealogy has not been just the domain of the privileged. In many traditional societies, it's taken very seriously because it helps embed individuals within a much larger network of relatives. *Clan*, which comes from a Gaelic word meaning children or progeny, was first used to describe the structure of society in the Scottish Highlands, where for many centuries your clan was a more important marker of identity than your immediate family. Many cultures across the world share this way of organizing society.

While most people today can trace their family back only a few generations, other cultures have been keeping track of their lineages for many hundreds of years. The Maori, the indigenous people of New Zealand, often know not only their lineage stretching back for generations but even the name of the canoe that brought their ancestors to their homeland eight centuries ago. The family tree of Confucius is said to be the oldest, stretching back more than 2,500 years and including more than two million members.

Genealogy is sometimes criticized for perpetuating class distinctions and encouraging snootiness. But a countervailing tendency in modern genealogy is the effort to connect with unusual ancestors, propriety be damned. If you can prove that you're descended from a person accused, tried, convicted, or executed for the practice of witchcraft prior to December 31, 1699, for example, you can join the Associated Daughters of Early American Witches. There's a society for the Descendants of the Illegitimate Sons and Daughters of the Kings of Britain, and one for people who can trace a connection to convicts transported to Australia between 1788–1869. The Society of Descendants of Lady Godiva welcomes those who can prove their connection to the famous lady with the long hair who lived in eleventh-century England. Go far enough back, and what was once seen as a scandal becomes merely colorful. My husband has a relative who was hanged as a horse thief in Wyoming, a fact that I've heard him brag about at least fifty times during the course of our marriage.

All of this is somewhat dampened by the fact that over enough generations, the genetic link becomes diluted. This is probably good news, given how fast ancestors pile up (going back sixteen generations, you have about 65,000 of them). As Christine Kenneally puts it in *The Invisible History of the Human Race: How DNA and History Shape Our Identities and Our Futures*, "If you built a time machine and traveled back four hundred years and . . . found yourself in a romance with one of your sixteenth-[great] grandmothers, the good news is that you can feel fine about having children together. However morally bizarre that might be, it would not be genetically problematic."

Academic historians tend to look down on the research methods of amateur genealogists, who may be sloppy in their sourcing (present company included). Just because you found a headstone with the right name on the Internet, in other words, doesn't mean it actually has your great-great-great-grandfather resting underneath it. At the same time, there's a growing recognition that the kind of microhistory done by genealogists can play a role in the larger effort to record and understand the past.

In my own case, I freely acknowledge the occasional sloppiness of my research. I'm pretty sure of my facts going back three generations, but after that most members of my family tree were added thanks to other people's work. I've made some efforts to double-check their information, but only until the records got murky and I gave up with a shrug. That's because I realized early in my efforts that what most interested me wasn't the begats but the stories. To me, the genetic information I'd gotten from AncestryDNA and the historical accuracy of my family tree weren't nearly as intriguing as the permission they gave me to let my imagination roam.

All of this got me thinking about my spiritual DNA. It wasn't a term I'd heard before, but if I had a genetic blueprint, why couldn't I have one relating to my spiritual identity as well? The idea expanded the standard definition of genealogy, making it a reflection of my soul's journey as much as the composition of my DNA. That genetic material was important in shaping me, to be sure, but equally important was the inspiration I've received from books, friendships, and stories, some contemporary and some millennia old. It felt natural to claim the authors of these influences as kin.

Because in the end, which is more important: our physical characteristics or our inner lives? Whether we can trace our ancestors back several centuries or whether we see ourselves as part of a long line of souls, each adding our individual spark to the flame of a much greater spirit? By adding these new elements to my genealogical quest, I felt like I'd opened the back of the wardrobe into Narnia.

I imagined a family tree filled not with the names of my relatives but instead with my spiritual heritage. Once again, starting with my name at the bottom, I went back one generation, filling in "God" in the box above mine. Being a good Trinitarian, I added Jesus and the Holy Spirit in adjacent boxes. And then I realized that because the Virgin Mary was Jesus' mom, her name should be entered on the next level up, making her my grandmother, as weird as that sounded.

Next came the Christian saints who've influenced me. I imagined St. Francis as a kindly, eccentric uncle (this would make him a brother of Jesus, but I didn't think either one of them would object to that). I added St. Columba, St. Teresa of Avila, and St. Hildegard of Bingen as first cousins. Martin Luther I penciled in as a second cousin—we'd seen each other a lot as children but had drifted apart through the years. The writer Thomas Merton certainly merited first cousin status as well, and activist Dorothy Day, too.

Venturing further afield, I started filling in more distant relatives. Buddhism was a branch of my family I hadn't even known existed until I was an adult. I penciled in some of its leading lights as third cousins. How wonderful to be able to claim a kinship with Siddhartha Gautama. That made the current Dalai Lama something on the order of a fifth cousin once removed—again, a pleasure.

By now I was really getting the hang of it, watching as my spiritual tree blossomed and expanded. I loved how the image made a similar point to that of DNA testing: we're all related. All spirit is connected, too. And everyone has a particular place on this vibrant network of energy that links us to a bigger web than we can possibly imagine.

There they were, my spiritual family, stretching over time and distance, bridging religions and traditions, all linked in a complex tangle of relationships. And once again, there I was, a little box at the bottom of the page, only this time it wasn't just all of human history that led to me but all of spiritual history as well.

I smiled. I quite liked doing spiritual genealogy.

CULTURAL COUSINS

My foray into spiritual genealogy made me realize that even conventional genealogy allows for more fluidity than we may think. Given the size of our family trees, all of us have some leeway in choosing which relatives we claim as kin. That's true not only for individual relatives, whether it's Leif Eriksson or Martin Luther King Jr., but also for entire cultures. In my case, I get to choose from among the marauding Vikings, the hardscrabble farmers of Norway and Iowa, and the upstanding modern Scandinavians. Given the increasing mixing of ethnicities—the growing numbers of Kenyans who marry Russians and Australians who marry Peruvians—many people have a far broader set of possibilities.

And who's to say you can't form a connection to another culture entirely, including people to whom you have no genetic link? I have a friend who's fallen in love with Italy, for example, who travels there, cooks its cuisine, listens to its operas, and has a *dolce vita* attitude toward life even though his family of origin is a particularly constipated product of the British Isles. Part of the glory of the modern world, in short, is that we're no longer tied to our ancestral identities. It used to be that if you were a baker, your son would be a baker too. If you were born in a small village in Eastern Europe, your great-grandchildren would likely still live in that village a century later. Today our options are nearly endless, which can bring its own set of challenges, but having to be a baker even if you're gluten-intolerant isn't one of them.

The question of how far this fluidity should go is a thorny one, however, because at a certain point cultural appreciation becomes cultural appropriation. I've never been personally offended when I see someone wearing a plastic Viking helmet with horns, despite its historical inaccuracy, but I can understand the philosophical issues this headgear raises. From restaurants that feature fluorescent Buddhas as part of their décor to college students wearing fake Indian warbonnets at Halloween, there's a slippery slope between admiring aspects of a culture and using it in inappropriate ways.

This point actually ties back to the spiritual realm, which has undergone its own revolutions relating to identity. In past centuries, religious identity was largely fixed, with Catholics producing Catholic babies who grew up to be Catholic parents, while Presbyterians and Methodists did the same in their denominational enclaves. But today in much of the world we're free to be any religion, or none at all, and many of us drop centuries of religious affiliation with hardly a backward glance. Others take on traditions rooted in cultures halfway across the globe, a phenomenon exceedingly rare for most of human history.

Considering that I've claimed the Dalai Lama as my fifth cousin, I shouldn't cast stones about spiritual appropriation. But I find it interesting that just as we celebrate our connections to certain relatives but not others, we pick our spiritual kindred spirits from a wide array of candidates. If you're a Catholic environmentalist, for example, you can choose Francis of Assisi, the brown-robed lover of animals from Italy, or Kateri Tekakwitha, the first Native American to be canonized as a saint. Both have been formally designated as patrons of ecology by the Roman Catholic Church. Or maybe you prefer a more recent spiritual mentor—perhaps Harriet Tubman or Ram Dass. Even if we don't share a genetic link with these people, we can forge a spiritual connection with them.

Whether it's conventional genealogy or my own quirky version of spiritual genealogy, the theoretical basis for my argument is the same: we're not just individuals, formed ex nihilo and living in pristine isolation. Instead, we're in relationship with those who've lived before us, reaching out to form connections with the dead in ways that help us live today. The Bible refers to the "great cloud of witnesses" that surrounds us. In my case, I like to imagine it includes my Aunt Vernelle, who's perched on the same billowy cloud as Sila, my Norwegian great-great-grandmother, while nearby is a bearded Viking who's looking a little bewildered by his conversation with the Virgin Mary. They're all part of the mix that makes me who I am.

A stained glass window at the Jorvik Viking Centre is based on a Viking Age illustration showing Norsemen leaving their ships to raid the east coast of England. (PHOTO BY BOB SESSIONS)

2

Badly Behaving Relatives

-·:❋:·-

During one long, brutal week in winter, I traveled with the Vikings. My time machine was a miserable case of the flu. Laid low by the virus, I tried to distract myself by binge-watching the History Channel's series *Vikings*. The show, set in eighth-century Scandinavia, follows the adventures of Ragnar Loth-brok, a farmer who becomes a Viking raider. With my mind befuddled by fever, the series morphed into a hallucinatory dream that became increasingly real as the days passed. One episode would end, and I'd immediately start another, anxious to learn what happened next. It might have been my Scandina-vian heritage, or it might have been the flu, but no matter—for that week I was a Viking.

I thrilled to the exploits of Ragnar, cheering when he defied the orders of his chieftain and made plans to go raiding in an undiscovered territory to the west. My heart leaped when I saw his new vessel sail into the fjord, a sleek longboat with an arched dragon head on its prow. I suffered with him and his crew on their long voyage into the unknown through fog, cold, and rain. ("I know how you feel," I told Ragnar from my supine position on the couch. "I'm miserable too.") I rejoiced when

31

they reached land, rooting for them as they sacked a monastery with brutal efficiency and then returned home with a ship full of treasure and captives. After they arrived back in their fjord, I was drawn into Ragnar's tangled web of relationships, trying to discern who was friend and who was foe. I especially admired Ragnar's fierce wife Lagertha, who could wield a weapon as powerfully as her husband. And when Ragnar faced his rival Earl Haraldson in hand-to-hand combat, I was riveted, my heart pounding with each jab and thrust of their swords.

In the midst of this Viking-induced mania, occasionally I'd resurface to find myself taken aback by my enjoyment of the carnage. I'd known the Viking Age was violent, but when viewed up close, the sheer scale of mayhem was both disconcerting and fascinating. So, for a palate cleanser, I'd occasionally switch to watching the American sitcom *The Office*, set in a paper company in Scranton, Pennsylvania. I'd laugh at the bumbling exploits of boss Michael Scott and cheer on the romance between the sweet receptionist Pam and her prank-loving boyfriend Jim.

Switching back and forth between the two series made for dizzying contrasts. First Ragnar and his crew returned to England to capture the king's brother and demand a ransom of 2,000 pounds of gold and silver; then salesman Dwight Schrute was given the responsibility for choosing the company's new health plan, leaving everyone dissatisfied because of the meagerness of its coverage. Ragnar ended up murdering his captive when the king refused to pay a ransom, while back at the office, the staff of Dunder Mifflin attended a Christmas party during which their gifts to fellow employees weren't well-received.

That schizophrenic week helped me understand why so many people are fascinated by the Vikings, even if they have no Scandinavian heritage. Most of us live in the world of *The Office*, with our days filled with petty dramas and small-scale concerns. We might worry about losing our jobs but not about losing our heads. The Vikings, however, as badly behaved as they often were, embody the thrill of a life on the edge, when making your way depended on courage, strength, and often violence.

Even after my fever ended and I returned to good health, the question remained. What do I really think about my ancestors the Vikings? And by extension, what should we all make of the less-than-savory elements of our ancestry?

I've long taken pride in being a descendant of the great explorer Leif Eriksson (his last name is spelled many ways, but I'll settle on this one). I've claimed this kinship on the basis of our shared Scandinavian ancestry, our mutual love of travel, our similar last names, and the fact that both of our first names start with an "L." In short, I'm just the sort of family-tree researcher who gives genealogy a bad name.

I've always considered Leif one of the good Vikings. No raiding and pillaging for him—instead he headed to North America around the year 1000 to found a new colony, leaving his home in Iceland to cross the stormy Atlantic at great risk. Somewhere in what is now Canada, he and his crew founded a settlement called Vinland. This was five centuries before Christopher Columbus landed in the Caribbean; a fact dwelled on at great length in my elementary-school classes in my Norwegian-American hometown. The contrast between the two explorers is stark: when Columbus encountered the native peoples, he enslaved them; when Leif faced hostility from the locals, he packed up and went back home. While Columbus carries a heavy weight of historical baggage, Leif is burdened with hardly any. His statue on the grounds of the Minnesota State Capitol shows him at his best: tall, virile, and handsome, the very model of a politically correct explorer.

My introduction to the less-reputable branches of the Viking clan came when I visited the British Isles a number of years before I started my roots quest. My husband, Bob, was the one who first noticed a disturbing pattern. We'd be touring a picturesque historic site when he'd look up from a guidebook and say, "Lori, here's *another* place that was a thriving community before your relatives attacked."

As we traveled, it became clear that my ancestors shared my attraction to holy sites, though in their case it wasn't because they were interested in deepening their prayer life. Instead they sought the wealth of Christian churches and monasteries, particularly their easily transportable gold and silver altarpieces. An added bonus was that such places were often poorly defended. A monk was no match for a warrior wielding a sword.

As we traveled, Bob and I had fun kidding each other about my bloodthirsty ancestors, but the reality of what the Vikings did was brought home to me during our visit to Lindisfarne in Northumberland. This peaceful spot on the northeast coast of England was once the site of a thriving monastery. Then, in 793, an attack on Lindisfarne began the Viking Age (the same raid portrayed in the TV series I'd watched while sick with the flu). The invaders plundered the monastery for treasures, took some of its monks as captives, killed others, and then disappeared in their boats. The assault on a renowned spiritual community shocked the European world.

As in the eighth century, today Lindisfarne is an island linked to the mainland by a causeway, which is covered by the tide twice a day. The sea is never far away, and as we wandered through its ruins and learned about its history, we could hear the rhythmic sweep of the waves and the calls of the seagulls—sounds little different, no doubt, from those heard by the monks on the morning of that fateful June day. It was easy to imagine their apprehension as they first saw the invaders approaching from the sea, and then their fear and terror as the Vikings started their deadly raid.

Near the end of our visit, we wandered into one of the modern buildings that cater to people who come here on pilgrimage. There we saw a small, framed letter on display: it was from the Norwegian government, and it contained a formal apology for what the Vikings had done twelve centuries before.

When I think back on my visit to Lindisfarne, it's that letter that sticks in my mind. I waver between thinking it honorable and viewing it as far too little and too late. And it brings to mind the central paradox of my ancestry. The Vikings were once the most-feared warriors in Europe, yet today Norway is universally admired for its harmonious society and well-functioning government. The country gives out the Nobel Peace Prize, for goodness sake. The Norwegians are the smiling, congenial relatives at the family reunion, the ones who talk about the weather and share homemade brownies, while in their attics they keep skeletons tucked away in ornately decorated trunks.

WARRIORS FROM THE NORTH

> "I have never seen more perfect physiques than theirs—they are like palm trees, are fair and reddish. . . . The man wears a cloak with which he covers one half of his body, leaving one of his arms uncovered. Every one of them carries an axe, a sword and a dagger."

The above description comes from Ibn Fadlan, an Arab writer who met Vikings along the Volga River in the tenth century while on a diplomatic mission from Baghdad. He went on to marvel at how each man was covered in tattoos from his toes to his neck and how the women wore fine jewelry of gold and silver that proclaimed their social status and the wealth of their husbands. He was less impressed by their hygiene habits ("indeed they are like wayward donkeys"), but their tall stature and striking good looks left a most memorable impression.

The Vikings made an impression, for good or ill, wherever they traveled. And travel they did, from the Arctic Circle to North Africa, from Baghdad and Constantinople to North America, their journeys taking them to nearly forty countries between the eighth and eleventh centuries. If you want to know why Scandinavian DNA shows up in your ancestry test, it's almost certainly due to the wanderlust of these people from the North.

The attack on Lindisfarne in 793 wasn't the first Viking raid, but it's considered the start of the Viking Age because it so galvanized the attention of Europe. At the time, Scandinavia was settled by a mix of tribal groups ruled by local chieftains. A growing population made land more valuable and prompted the adventurous, restless, and ambitious to look abroad, where treasure stolen on raids could buy land, power, and status or fund a bride price so that a Viking warrior could marry. Gold and silver were easily transported and stored, making them much more convenient to trade than livestock or land. While the Vikings were at times brutal, it was a violent time all over Europe. The collapse of the Roman Empire had shifted the power balance between peoples and led to a breakdown of law and order in many places. Even churches sometimes engaged in warfare, with much jockeying for position between rivals.

At first the raids were small scale, consisting of just a few boats, but over the centuries they increased greatly in size. When Vikings laid siege to Paris in 845, they had a flotilla of 120 ships; when they attacked Constantinople in 907, they had two thousand. For three centuries they dominated the consciousness of Europe; even if you hadn't been attacked, the threat was always out there, particularly if you lived close to water.

The classic image of Vikings is of helmeted warriors from the mountains and fjords of Norway, setting out in dragon-headed boats to raid the coasts of England and Ireland. But there were also Vikings from the flatter lands of Sweden and Denmark (though those national boundaries would come later). They weren't just raiders, either, but also merchants, engineers, colonizers, mercenaries, and explorers. They were the consummate opportunists, constantly on the lookout for their next lucky break, whether it came through friendly or violent means. Depending on how you squint at the historical record, they were either warrior merchants or merchant warriors.

The word *Viking* comes from the Old Norse *vikingr*, meaning raider or pirate. It could also be used as a verb: to go *a-viking* meant to venture out seeking wealth. Most Scandinavians of the day were not Vikings but instead poor farmers who scraped out a precarious existence. A more accurate term for Scandinavians during this period is the Norse, though in modern-day parlance we tend to call them all Vikings, which is a disservice to the majority of people who stayed home and behaved themselves (in fact, perhaps no more than 5 or 10 percent of the Norse participated in raiding). And even those who were true Vikings often had raiding as a part-time occupation, which they did during the summer months after the crops were planted—similar to schoolteachers today who do painting jobs during the summer to make extra money, only with swords.

The Vikings went *a-viking* to different regions, depending on where their homeland was. From Denmark, they sailed primarily to England, where they made money both by raiding and from protection money, which local rulers paid in huge sums to keep them away. One indication of how successful they were is that archaeologists have found six times as many medieval English coins in Scandinavia as they have in England. The Vikings of western Norway, meanwhile, headed to Ireland and Scotland, including the Shetland and Orkney Islands, which they dominated for seven centuries. Many of the residents of the islands to this day have closer cultural ties to Norway than to Great Britain.

By the height of the Viking Age, the Norse roamed all over mainland Europe, using its rivers as their highways. Because theirs was primarily an oral culture, much of what we know about them comes from the people they raided, whose accounts of them are hardly unbiased. Appearing off the coastline without warning, they struck with brutal swiftness and then left before defenses could be mounted.

What made the raiders of the North so devastating sprang in large part from their ships. The people of Scandinavia had long been adept at ship building, but during the seventh century they developed a new style of vessel, warships that were long and sleek, with upward-thrusting prows at either end. Men scoured the forests to find trees with just the right curve and then further shaped the wood to precisely fit their needs. Using axes, they took advantage of the natural grain of the wood to give the planks optimal flexibility and strength. A single mast up to 60 feet tall stood in the center of each boat, carrying as much as 1,000 square feet of sail. The crew (who typically numbered between thirty and eighty men) could also row as needed, their overlapping shields arranged on the sides of the boat.

Viking shipwrights made technological improvements that included a keel, a kind of backbone for the boat formed from the wood of a single tree. The boat itself was built with overlapping planks of wood, which allowed the vessel to flex in rough seas. A Viking warship could travel up to 15 knots (about 17 miles per hour) and navigate even small rivers. In the hands of skilled sailors, the Viking longboats were so maneuverable that they were said to be almost alive.

And as if all these innovations weren't enough, the Viking longboats had dragon's heads on the prows, which they believed protected them from evil spirits. The animals' coiled necks and piercing gaze could be seen from a long distance, announcing the fact that the boat was filled with equally fierce and bold warriors. It's no wonder the people who lived by the sea and along rivers were terrified by the sight of them.

As traders, however, the Norse had a less confrontational approach. Swedish Vikings crossed the Baltic Sea and then wound their way by river through dense forests to reach large trading centers such as Constantinople and Baghdad, where they sold luxury goods that included furs, walrus ivory, and amber. Some became settlers on the way, giving up their wandering ways to make new homes with wives and families they'd brought with them from Scandinavia. The Norse had such a strong influence on the lands to the east that the word Russia may be derived from *Rus*, the name of a tribe of Swedish Vikings. *Rus* itself is related to the Old Norse word for "rower," referring to men who rowed boats. Many Russians continue to take pride in their Viking heritage, viewing it as one of the wellsprings of strength in their history.

In Constantinople, the Vikings so impressed the Byzantine emperors that they recruited them for their elite bodyguard, the Varangian Guards. Partly it was because of their fighting prowess and impressive physical presence, but their outsider status also made them less susceptible to corruption and the political intrigues of the court. The Viking graffiti that I saw in

Hagia Sophia might well have been scratched into the marble by one of these guards, taking a break from his duties while the emperor worshiped.

THE ENGLISH VIKINGS

The tunic-clad, bearded man who greeted me at the entrance to the Jorvik Viking Centre in the English city of York seemed oddly genial for a Viking. "Wait just a minute, luv, for these ladies to enter," he said to me, waving through a group of white-haired pensioners in front of me.

Amused by his politeness, I wondered how a real Viking warrior would have reacted when a group of strangers tried to enter his home. It wouldn't take much to rob the entire lot of us, though some of the women in the group ahead of me did look like they could wield an umbrella with considerable force.

Jorvik draws visitors from around the world because it's one of the best-preserved Viking Age settlements ever found. Archaeologists discovered it under the streets of a neighborhood in York in the 1970s. Over several years they gradually uncovered houses, workshops, and backyards dating back to the tenth century. Thousands of items were recovered, from pottery shards and pieces of jewelry to organic remains, ones that typically decay quickly but which were unusually well-preserved by the moist and peaty soil of the area. Textiles, timbers, animal bones, seeds, pollen, plants, and parasite eggs gave researchers insights into the diet and health of Jorvik's residents and the climate of the region.

Ivar the Boneless gets the credit for bringing the Vikings to this part of England. (The Norse often gave brutally honest nicknames to their leaders, and Ivar's name refers either to a physical disability or to his lack of prowess in bed.) Beginning in 866, Ivar conquered much of northern England, leading a group of warriors that the native Anglo-Saxons called the Great Heathen Army. After years of warfare, the country was divided into a southern kingdom ruled by Anglo-Saxon kings and a northern region called the Danelaw controlled by the Vikings. Jorvik became its capital city and an important trade hub linked to the rest of the Viking world.

After the completion of the dig, the Jorvik Viking Centre was created to tell about the remarkable discoveries made here. Its first room has a glass floor that allowed me to peer into a recreation of the building foundations of a Norse neighborhood from ten centuries ago. Seeing the modest size of the homes and how closely they were packed together, I concluded that the Vikings certainly weren't living in luxury in Jorvik, at least according to modern-day standards.

A guide dressed in Viking attire gave me a more nuanced picture. People came here from throughout the Norse world to trade, visit, and settle, he said. They spoke multiple languages and bartered goods that included walrus tusks from the Arctic, silks from Asia, and amber from the Baltics. They were craftsmen, too, creating wooden cups and bowls, metal objects such as knives and jewelry, and leather goods.

Hearing his enthusiasm for the topic, I asked about his own background. He told me that he was an actor by training and had been hired as a performer during the Jorvik Viking Festival that's held each February. That experience made him curious about the history of the Norse, sparking a fascination that led to his current job. I told him about having contracted my own version of the Viking bug, then asked him what interested him most about the Norse.

"I'm intrigued by the mysteriousness of the Viking Age and by how much we still don't know about them," he said. "And I think this site is especially interesting because of the blend of cultures here. These were pagan Vikings living among Anglo-Saxon Christians, and they traded with people all over the known world. In some ways this site is just ordinary streets and homes with nothing grand about them at all, but once you start digging into the details, an entire world comes to life."

In the next exhibit, I boarded a gondola-like car that took me right into the middle of that world: a Jorvik neighborhood that's been recreated using information gleaned from the archaeological dig, complete with animatronic figures, thatched-roof buildings, realistic-looking mud and grime, and piped-in smells that included the unmistakable odor of manure.

Though it was a bit cheesy, a sort of Disney-theme-park-of-the-Middle-Ages, as I glided through the streets, I couldn't help but be swept up in the illusion of traveling back in time. I nodded my head in greeting when a hunter hailed a welcome in Old Norse and then observed other residents of the neighborhood at work and leisure, including an Arabic trader selling silks, a blacksmith teaching his son how to sharpen a knife, a couple of fishermen discussing their catch of the day, and a woman walking slowly with a crutch (her skeleton, I learned later, showed that she had a degenerative joint disease). If you gave these people a bath, shaved the men, and put them in modern dress, they wouldn't look much different from the people walking the streets of York today.

Stepping out of the time machine, I next toured a gallery that displayed some of the actual artifacts found at the site, which ranged from a cowrie shell from the Red Sea and skates made from horse leg bones to a piece of fossilized Viking poop displayed in a lighted case like it was a precious jewel (historians get excited about the darndest things). I can now report that while many things have changed in the past thousand years, human excrement is not one of them.

Another display, however, gave me an idea of just how different my world was from that of the Vikings. An interpreter showed me a Norse comb made of deer antler and then a modern recreation of it that had been crafted by a staff member. "It took him a hundred hours," she said. "It's no wonder combs were luxury items during the Viking Age." That explained the hairstyles of those who lived in the Jorvik neighborhood, I thought, peering at the item with interest. I would never look at a cheap plastic comb in the same way again.

But to me the most intriguing display was on the Middleton Cross, a tenth-century grave marker found about thirty miles from York. While its shape is clearly Christian, on one side it has a well-armed Viking warrior and, on the other side, a serpent that's thought to represent the dragon Nidhogg that gnaws at the foot of the world tree Yggdrasil. Above both figures are the interlaced ribbons that are common in Scandinavian designs. The markings reflect the fact that many of the Vikings in York eventually became Christian, despite their comrades' fondness for raiding monasteries. I imagined the Viking family that had ordered the carving of the original cross. "Put something on it to honor Dad," they said. "He so loved going into battle."

The final displays in the museum completed the story of the Norse in the north of England. Around 954, Eric Bloodaxe, the last Viking king in Jorvik, was defeated by the King of Wessex from the south. The final expulsion of the Vikings from England came in 1066, when their army was defeated by the Saxons at the Battle of Stamford Bridge eight miles from York—though by that time many Vikings had intermarried with the locals and were well-integrated into the city that their ancestors had conquered. They would remain while their comrades returned to the homeland.

Just three weeks after the defeat of those Vikings, William the Conqueror (himself of Viking stock) became king of England at the Battle of Hastings, an event that is generally thought to mark the end of the Viking Age. After that, the Norse stayed home, their raiding days behind them for a variety of reasons. Most European countries now had standing armies to defend themselves. Isolated outposts invested in fortifications, and some of the oh-so-tempting-to-raid monasteries just gave up and moved inland. Some Vikings became Christian and were told by their priests that raiding wasn't an appropriate career choice anymore. And in many places they simply blended into the local scene. In France they became Normans, a word that derives from *North-men*. In the British Isles they intermarried with the native English, Irish, Welsh, and Scottish—though I suspect that when an especially tall, strapping, blond-haired lad towered over his mates, there were some who felt an instinctual raising of the hair on the back of their necks.

The Viking influence lingers to this day both in England and in the English language. The many towns in the north of England ending in *-thorpe, -ness, -kirk, -keld,* and *–thwaite* bear witness to their Norse origins. And Jorvik (which is pronounced "your-vik" in Old Norse) later became York, which in turn lent its name to New York in the United States. Those who walk beneath its gleaming skyscrapers are linked by history to the smelly streets of Jorvik.

Our language bears witness to these Viking colonizers as well, because hundreds of Old Norse words became part of English. Some clearly reflect Viking predilections and preoccupations, from *berserk,* which comes from "bear shirt," a reference to the furs that warriors often wore into battle, to *ransack, club, knife, slaughter, anger, die, rotten,* and *ugly.* But there are kinder, gentler Viking words as well, from *husband* and *skill* to *thrift,* plus indispensable ordinary words that include *skin, sky, ball,* and *leg.*

Like the Norse neighborhood that lies underneath the streets of modern-day York, the influence of the Vikings is part of our cultural heritage, waiting to be discovered if we dig deep enough.

OUTLAW KIN

As I pondered my visit with the Vikings of York, I kept coming back to the most disturbing thing I saw in the recreated neighborhood in Jorvik: a slave woman with bound hands. Her plight made me reflect on the larger problem of what to do with badly behaving relatives in genealogy. Being related to the colorful and scandalous is one thing (think of those societies for the illegitimate offspring of British royalty or accused witches, for example), but ties to the cruel and barbarous are quite another. Unfortunately, we all have them in our family trees—the slave traders and mob bosses, the murderers and embezzlers, the ones who succeeded by violence and graft and all-around nastiness. Even relatives who belong to a political party different from ours may elicit heartburn. Linked to us by blood alone, they're people we'd hesitate to invite in the door if they arrived on our front step.

I'm lucky in that most of my nefarious relatives lived a thousand years ago (though I must admit to being a little sorry that the wealth they'd accumulated from raiding has long since evaporated). Instead, my more immediate ancestors were poor farmers eking out a living in Norway and rural Iowa. They were quiet and circumspect, people who thought that standing out in any way was a serious breach of propriety. If my clan had a family motto, it would be *Quid Cogitant* (Latin for "What would they think?")—a far cry indeed from the wild warriors of the North.

But even though the Vikings lived many centuries ago, meaning that my own genetic connection to them is admittedly tenuous, as I began to research my family history, I realized I needed to face some hard truths. I admired much about them—their courage and strength, their sense of adventure and chameleon-like ability to adapt to whatever circumstances they found themselves in—but their darker side is undeniable.

Their participation in the slave trade, especially, is well documented. Ever the shrewd businessmen, on their raids Norsemen often captured people either for their own use or to sell. These unlucky souls became *thralls*, an Old Norse word for slave (the phrase "to be enthralled" contains an echo of this meaning). Thralls built ships, wove cloth, cared for children, tended crops and animals, and satisfied the sexual desires of their owners. Some women enjoyed a slightly better fate when they became the wives of Viking men, who would choose mates from among their captives when there was a shortage of females in their home territories. But having to marry the person who'd abducted you from your home, of course, wasn't an enviable fate either.

One of the most compelling stories about a Viking slave comes from the Arab explorer Ibn Fadlan, the man who admired the physiques of the Vikings he encountered along the Volga River. In the 920s, he observed the burial of a chieftain in what is now Russia. Ibn Fadlan's long and detailed description conveys his fascinated horror at the proceedings. He recounts that after a slave girl "volunteered" to be sacrificed, she was plied with alcohol and forced to have sex with the chieftain's friends. Then she was led by a woman (appropriately called the Angel of Death) to a pavilion where the chieftain's body lay. After she entered the enclosure, men standing outside beat their shields so that her screams couldn't be heard as two men throttled her neck with a rope and the woman stabbed her repeatedly. Then the bodies of the girl and her master, along with a half-dozen sacrificed animals and an array of weapons, clothing, and furs, were placed inside a boat that had been pulled up on the shore. As a crowd watched, the entire lot was set ablaze.

It's sobering to realize that this is an example of Vikings on their *best* behavior at a funeral. It was a violent age, to be sure, and there were even worse cultural and religious practices in those days, but the story is still a reminder that we shouldn't romanticize the Vikings. Even after a thousand years, their actions have the power to shock us.

My uneasiness with parts of my heritage is hardly unique. Many people struggle to come to terms with the disreputable and sometimes evil doings of their ancestors. The close relatives of Adolf Hitler, for example, reportedly made a pact not to have children because they didn't want to continue the genetic inheritance of one of history's worst dictators. Others have learned that their ancestors were involved with organized crime, participated in genocide, or were mass murderers.

In the United States, many have been shocked to discover that their relatives kept slaves or participated in the transport of captives from Africa, knowledge that for too long was either ignored, denied, or minimized in genealogical research. Increasingly people are acknowledging the harsh reality of what was done by some of their forebears and are working to find ways to help atone for historical wrongs.

Genealogy, in short, makes it difficult to claim the moral high ground. If we go far enough back, all of us have many examples of both the oppressed and the oppressor in our lineages (and sometimes, of course, they were both, as people who are abused tend to abuse others when they get the chance). It's hard enough for contemporary people to keep out of ethical quagmires, but the brutal realities of life during most of human history meant that one's survival often depended on cruelty and violence. Slavery, in particular, wound its poisonous way through many cultures, from ancient Greece and the Ottoman Empire to the Aztecs and Mayans of Central America. Even today, millions of people around the world continue to live in bondage as victims of human trafficking—and the descendants of those perpetrating this evil will one day have to come to terms with their legacy.

A tendency to smaller-scale misbehaviors can also run in families. From alcoholism to abuse, destructive patterns often pass from generation to generation. While it can be disheartening to realize you come from a long line of people who've struggled with addiction or perpetuated abuse, it can also be liberating. Knowledge, after all, is power. Multiple forms of dysfunction may have existed for generations in your family, but those destructive patterns can stop with you. And while it's nice to find ancestors who served in the French Resistance or who were part of the Underground Railroad, sometimes the best thing that can come from genealogical research is a clear view of all the crap that's accumulated in the clan over the centuries, floating like turds in the family gene pool.

If you want to climb onto a perch from which you can judge the rest of the world's iniquity, in other words, then genealogy is not the hobby for you. Research on the twists and turns of our lineages reinforces the perennial truth that within all of us is the potential for good and evil. Given the right circumstances—economic hardship, war, disease, and famine—we too may compromise, cheat, or commit violence.

"The line separating good and evil passes not through states, nor between classes, nor between political parties either—but right through every human heart," wrote Aleksandr Solzhenitsyn, who, having suffered through the Soviet Gulag, knew very well the truth of which he spoke.

When we ponder our family trees, some humility is required.

A statue of the Norse explorer Leif Eriksson stands in the Canadian village of L'Anse aux Meadows. (PHOTO BY BOB SESSIONS)

3

A Norse Soap Opera

-»:❋:«-

I remember the shock I experienced the first time I met someone who was unfamiliar with Leif Eriksson. I'd grown up in a community in which he was one of our ancestral superstars, though in the modest culture of small-town Iowa that didn't mean you could get too boastful about him. Still, there was a street named after him; the high school athletic teams were the Vikings; and a local museum told the story of the Norwegians who came to America, including Leif, who led the way. I even had a great uncle named Leif Erickson, though I met him only once because he inexplicably moved to Canada, showing a wanderlust in keeping with his namesake, but not with the rest of our stay-at-home relatives.

I realized how far outside that enclave I'd wandered when I encountered a woman who didn't understand my reference to my illustrious ancestor. "Leif who?" she asked.

I was embarrassed for her. How could you *not* know about Leif Eriksson? He was the first European to land in North America and one of the world's most famous Scandinavians. Had she never heard of Leif Eriksson Day, celebrated each year on October 9? It wasn't a big holiday, I had to admit, but it was still officially designated by the U.S. Congress (the date was chosen because that's when the first of the nineteenth-century Norwegian immigrants arrived in New York in 1825). Norwegian Americans don't brag about much—it's just not in our makeup—but if we're proud of anyone, it's Leif Eriksson. The serendipitous fact that my name sort of matched his was a source of pride for me from the time I was small. Also, I didn't have any other famous relatives, and you go with what you have.

As I grew older, however, my pride in the connection waned, especially when I realized how far out of fashion he'd fallen in the larger culture. He was, after all, very white, very male, and very dead. In the debate over whether to rename Columbus Day as Indigenous Peoples' Day, for example, no one ever brought up Leif as a compromise. And other than setting foot in North America, I wasn't sure what else he'd done.

But as I dove deeper into my genealogical research, I wanted to go further back than I could get on Ancestry.com—back to a man and a family who lived in a world very different from my own. By learning about his life and the spiritual forces that shaped him, I hoped to find answers to some of my own existential questions.

CHRONICLES OF THE NORTH

We know about Leif Eriksson thanks to the Icelandic sagas, a body of literature that is to the Icelanders what Homer's *Odyssey* is to the Greeks. The sagas, written three centuries after the events they chronicle, blend fact and fiction, history and myth. While they at times veer into folklore (trolls, anyone?), they also have a shaggy-headed authenticity about them, with a hint of a chill north wind wafting from each page.

To understand the sagas, some national genealogy is required. On the family tree of Scandinavia, Norway is the grandparent, Iceland the child, Greenland the grandchild, and Newfoundland the great-grandchild. That's how Norse

explorers leapfrogged across the islands of the North beginning in the ninth century. First a group of Norwegians settled
Iceland, traveling across the sea to homestead a land even more
windswept and rugged than their homeland. In the tenth century, a group of Icelanders headed farther west to Greenland.
They were fortunate to do so during a period when the tem-
peratures were warmer than they are now, but life was still
harsh. Even at its height, the colony in Greenland probably
numbered fewer than three thousand people, though they nevertheless had enough wanderlust to mount four expeditions
to a place called Vinland in what was likely Newfoundland.
These colonies met with different levels of success. In Iceland
the immigrants took root, creating what became a kind of
Wild West of Scandinavia, but the other settlements would
eventually fail, Greenland after four centuries and Vinland
after just a decade.

The Icelandic sagas were written in the thirteenth and fourteenth centuries, but they were based on an oral tradition that
stretched back much further. In describing the exploits of the
men and women who settled Iceland, Greenland, and Vinland,
they're full of dramatic stories and epic confrontations, feuds
and betrayals, tragedy and romance. Their conversations and
descriptions are so vivid that literary scholars consider them
precursors of the modern novel. They were written by Christians, who were motivated in part by a desire to record cau-
tionary tales of how violent the Icelanders were before they
got right with Jesus. But we sense, too, hints of admiration for
their larger-than-life pagan ancestors.

The history of the Vinland expeditions is told mainly in *The
Saga of Erik the Red* and *The Saga of the Greenlanders*. While
there are variations between the two stories, their outlines are
similar, suggesting that their authors used a common oral tradition. In recounting the story here, I'll blend details from the
two sagas, hoping that in the mix the truth emerges in rough
form. The two sagas are short, taking just a few hours to read,
but they pack a lot of action into their pages. And the more I
read, the more Leif seemed less like an exemplar of all that was

dignified and impressive in Norwegian culture and more like a character in a Norse soap opera.

Consider his father, Erik the Red, standing tall and strong with a full beard and thick head of red hair. He was brave and smart but also had, as we say today, an anger-management problem. Born in Norway, he was forced to leave his homeland "because of some killings," a shrug-of-the-shoulders phrase that indicates that well, these things happen, don't they, and we shouldn't make too big a deal of them. After settling in Iceland, he had a falling out with his neighbors and ended up killing several of them (but since they'd mistreated some of his slaves, the implication is that he was somewhat justified). Erik the Red was banished again—by now he must have been used to it—and was told that he couldn't return to Iceland for three years.

Erik made good use of his time in exile. He sailed to a land that lay to the west, an island that had been spotted some years before by Vikings who'd been blown off course. He explored its coast and inlets, searching for the right place to establish a colony. When he returned to Iceland, he announced that he'd found a splendid new place called Greenland, a name he chose because it sounded attractive, even though most of the land was snow covered. He convinced other households to follow him and founded his own estate in a prime spot of land called Brattahlid, meaning "steep slope."

Erik and his wife Thjodhild had four children, who were a mixed lot in terms of temperament and ability to stay on the right side of the law. One son was Leif, known as Eriksson for obvious reasons. His sister was Freydis, a domineering woman who'd married a feckless man "mainly for his money," as the author of the Greenlanders' saga says with a sniff of disapproval. The other two children were Thorvald and Thorstein, monikers that illustrate the fact that in Scandinavia then and for many centuries later, including a reference to the god Thor in a name was a smart bit of cheap insurance.

While Erik the Red was a mixed bag, ethics-wise, Leif is described only in laudatory terms. He was large and strong, the sagas say, of striking appearance and wise and kind. He was also "a man of moderation in all things," a description not often applied to Vikings. Leif sailed to Norway, where he became one of King Olaf Tryggvason's men and converted to Christianity. The king told him to return to Greenland to persuade the heathens there to adopt the new faith. Leif agreed to do his best, though he said his efforts would likely meet a harsh reception in Greenland, no doubt thinking of his father, Erik the Red, who'd been kicked out of two countries for murder. Leif's proselytizing turned out to be quite successful, however, and many in the colony converted to the new faith, though his crusty sire was reluctant to give up his pagan ways, even after his wife became a Christian and refused to sleep with him unless he converted.

Leif then hatched a plan to search for new territories to the west of Greenland. This land had been spotted several years before by a merchant whose ship had been blown off course (this happened a lot during this era, given the fact that the North Atlantic is one of the most dangerous stretches of sea in the world and the Norse lacked modern navigational tools). Erik at first planned to go along, until he fell from a horse on his way to the boat, injuring his foot. "I'm not meant to be part of the expedition," he concluded, and he stayed at home in Greenland, thus missing his chance to be a famous explorer.

Setting out with a crew of thirty-four men, Leif began a long and dangerous voyage. After weeks of sailing, they first passed by a land filled with rocks (possibly Baffin Island) and then one with trees (probably Labrador). At last they reached a more congenial landscape, where the rivers ran thick with salmon and the pastures were lush. Leif called the new land Vinland, meaning Wineland, because it had wild grapes growing in abundance on its shores. The crew built a set of longhouses, which they used as a base for deeper explorations into the region.

Returning to Greenland the next spring, Leif became wealthy from the timber and grapes they'd brought back from Vinland. He was known as Leif the Lucky because he'd rescued a boatload of people stranded at sea (including a woman who'd turn out to be significant for both his story and mine). And after the death of his father, he became chieftain.

The description of Leif's own family leaves us hungry for more details. According to the sagas, he had two sons. Thorgils was the child of Thorgunna from the Scottish Hebrides, a woman he met when his ship was—you guessed it—blown off course traveling between Greenland and Norway. "Thorgils was thought to have something preternatural about him," says the saga writer with intriguing vagueness—exactly what was so unnerving about him is never explained. Leif's other son, Thorkell, who was apparently normal, succeeded him as chieftain of the Greenland settlement.

Thus ends the story of Leif Eriksson. He fades into the mist of a Scandinavian winter, ending his days most likely in Greenland, unaware that he would eventually end up as a statue on the grounds of the Minnesota State Capitol, a symbol of all that's strong and admirable in Scandinavian culture.

But there's another member of his family whose story is told in much greater detail: his sister-in-law, Gudrid, whom I'd discovered during my fortuitous bathroom break in Iceland. While Leif comes off as a bit stiff and bland, Gudrid strides out of the pages of the sagas like the heroine of a movie.

A WOMAN WHO KNEW HOW
TO BEHAVE AROUND STRANGERS

One evening during a bitterly cold winter in Greenland, a young woman is asked to summon the spirits. Even by Greenland standards, it's been a terrible winter. The men have had bad luck hunting, and some haven't returned at all from their expeditions. Illness stalks the community. A shipwreck has brought additional mouths to feed, straining the food stores even more.

A famed seeress named Thorbjorg is invited to visit. She's the only remaining sibling of a family of ten sisters, all of whom shared the same uncanny ability to predict the future. She makes an appropriately grand entrance, coming in from the frigid outdoors in dramatic fashion. Dressed in a black mantle adorned with precious stones, she has a hood of black lambskin lined with white cat-skin and leather gloves and boots lined with fur. She carries a staff topped with a brass ornament and ornamental stones, and around her neck is a string of imported glass beads. At her waist is a belt from which hangs a purse that holds her magical charms.

That night Thorbjorg eats a meal that includes all the best foods the farm can scrape together, including the hearts of various animals, which she eats with her own set of finely made cutlery. The farmer, obsequious in the face of her splendor, asks this mysterious guest of honor when she thinks she might have some answers to their questions about the future. "Let me sleep on it," she says, keeping them all in suspense for another day.

At last, late in the afternoon, the time comes for Thorbjorg's prophecies. The residents of the farm prepare a high seat for her topped by a cushion stuffed with chicken feathers, instead of the straw or grass used by people of more lowly station. Before ascending to it, she lays out her charms and the various items provided for her (they're not specified, but we can imagine they're the equivalent of eye of newt and toe of frog). But there's a problem: she needs a woman to chant the magical incantations that will summon the spirits.

One of the shipwrecked visitors, a young woman named Gudrid, pipes up. "I don't have magical powers or the gift of prophecy," she says, "but in Iceland my foster-mother, Halldis, taught me songs for summoning spirits."

Thorbjorg invites her to start singing, but Gudrid demurs. "I'm a Christian woman and it wouldn't be right for me to sing these songs," she says, making us wonder why she spoke up in the first place.

Just when you think Gudrid is a hopeless goody-two shoes, she changes her mind, in part because she's encouraged by the farmer, who clearly wants to see a return on his investment in asking Thorbjorg to visit. The sorceress climbs up on the platform prepared for her, and a group of women form a protective ring around her. All eyes turn toward Gudrid, who's been described earlier in the tale as "the most attractive of women." She was probably blond, and I like to think tall too, with a bit of a Valkyrie air about her.

I wish I could have witnessed the moment when Gudrid began singing. I can imagine the scene: the wind howling outside, the crackling of the fire, the darkness pressing close all around. The people's faces are intent and serious, waiting for what will happen next, eager to hear hopeful words that will give them strength to get through this hard time. It's a scene poised between the pagan and Christian worlds, between the realm of magic and the annals of history.

Gudrid does not disappoint them. She chants so beautifully that people said they'd never heard the songs sung in a fairer voice. Her foster mother had taught her well: a spell is woven. The sorceress feels the spirits arrive, drawn to Gudrid's voice. She finally has all she needs to work her magic. "Many things are now clear to me that were hidden before," Thorbjorg says.

Even better, the news brought by the spirits is good. The time of hardship will last no longer, and good times will return. The bout of illness will recede. Then she turns to give a message to Gudrid, probably surprising her with the direct address. "You will make the most honorable of matches," she tells her. "From you will be descended a long and worthy line. Over all the branches of your family a bright ray will shine."

The scribe who recorded this tale was a Christian, writing centuries later. No doubt he'd been repeatedly warned about the dangers of paganism. And Gudrid was the ancestor of prominent bishops in Iceland, who had a vested interest in having a devout foremother. But still, the story was too good to leave out. Just when the seeress needed a helper, Gudrid stepped up with an offer of a pagan song. And even from a distance of a thousand years, we can still hear a hint of its melody.

Ever since I encountered her statue in a roadside park in Iceland, the story of Gudrid the Far Traveler has fascinated me. I was surprised I'd never heard of her before. While her brother-in-law Leif was famous, at least in Scandinavian circles, Gudrid's story is equally remarkable—in the Vinland sagas, in fact, she gets more attention than Leif does. She was "a woman who knew how to behave around strangers," which is certainly a good characteristic to have if you want to explore new lands. Of both Norwegian and Irish heritage, she was born on the Snæfellsnes Peninsula around 985 (near the roadside park where I'd seen her statue). The daughter of a wealthy farmer, she spent part of her youth living with foster parents who were friends of her father. As a young woman, she traveled to Greenland on a boat that ran into trouble and was rescued by Leif Eriksson, the incident that earned him the nickname Lucky.

The details of her story vary somewhat between *The Saga of Erik the Red* and *The Saga of the Greenlanders*, but both agree that in Greenland she married Leif's brother, Thorstein. In one version of the story, the two of them set out for the mysterious lands to the west of Greenland, got lost, and spent all summer being tossed about by the sea. Back in Greenland, Thorstein took ill and died—though shortly after his death his corpse sat up in bed and prophesied, like the seeress did, that Gudrid would have a long life with many descendants. When people saw Gudrid, apparently they just couldn't help themselves from predicting good things for her.

Then she married again, this time to a wealthy merchant named Thorfinn Karlsefni (from here on I'm going to call him by his last name to distinguish him from all the other people with Thor-names). Despite having spent a miserable summer sailing around in circles in the fog, rain, and cold looking for new lands to the west, Gudrid convinced him to mount another expedition. The two of them put together a crew of sixty men and five women. While the goal of Leif's expedition had been primarily to gather products to sell back home, Gudrid and Karlsefni intended to establish a colony in Vinland. This time the voyage was successful, and they sailed without incident to the spot where Leif and his men had built longhouses, which they used as a home base (Leif, ever the savvy businessman, said that he wouldn't give the houses to them, but he'd *lend* them).

According to the sagas, their lives were good there. Gudrid gave birth to a son named Snorri, who despite his name wasn't one of the Seven Dwarves but instead the first child of European heritage born in North America. The land was rich in natural bounty, from grapes to fish and game, and they also had meat and milk and cheese from their own livestock.

Then came their first encounter with the native people of the area, whom the Norse called Skraelings. During that visit, the two groups exchanged goods amicably, trading furs and animal skins for milk products, which the natives had likely never tasted. But the second visit had a much different outcome. One of the Skraelings tried to take one of the settler's weapons and was killed in the skirmish. A battle ensued, during which many of the natives were killed.

During this drama-filled episode, there was a quiet interaction much different in character. As Gudrid was sitting inside one of the houses with her baby, a Skraeling woman approached her. The two of them tried to find a way to communicate despite having no common language.

"My name is Gudrid," said Gudrid, making a motion for the woman to sit down.

"My name is Gudrid," repeated the woman.

It's just the sort of detail that seems authentic. That's how communication works when you have no words in common— you repeat the words of the other person. Gudrid did indeed know how to behave around strangers, and the other woman was eager to connect with her as well. Unfortunately, their friendly interaction didn't last long. When they heard sounds of fighting in the distance, the native woman disappeared.

After that conflict with the Skraelings, the settlers stayed through the winter with no further encounters. But in the spring Karlsefni made the decision to return to Greenland. The Vinland colony was small and vulnerable, far from any help from their homeland, and the Skraelings would undoubtedly return, probably with a much larger force. So the Norse packed up their belongings and left.

In my mind's eye I can see Gudrid standing on the deck of a boat, watching as the place where she thought she'd spend the rest of her life grows smaller and smaller. She holds her young son in her arms, knowing that he'll remember nothing of the land of his birth. We don't know if she felt regret; maybe she was happy to be going back to Greenland. But from all we know of Gudrid the Far Traveler, I doubt it. She'd tried so hard and sacrificed so much to get to Vinland. She was an explorer and a risk taker, an equal partner with her husband in adventure. But now it was time to say goodbye. She watches for a long time, standing there until nothing of her home is visible, and then at last she turns around to face forward.

ANCESTRAL GUIDES

It's not hard to see why I'm attracted to Gudrid. Like her, I consider myself a far traveler, though my own journeys have been much easier. Intelligent, kind, and resourceful, she was also "one to be reckoned with in all her dealings," according to *The Saga of Erik the Red*, which is as fine a description of a formidable and capable person as I can imagine. Think of her bravery in heading to Vinland with Karlsefni—she'd already nearly lost her life twice at sea, once when she was shipwrecked and the other time when she and her first husband spent a summer sailing around in circles in the North Atlantic. But her dream of heading to unknown lands persisted. Leif gets all the glory in the history books, but Gudrid was a hero too.

Gudrid is a prime example of how you want to be picky in choosing your ancestral role models. Don't settle for the second-rate: choose someone remarkable. With all of human history at your disposal—or at least your segment of its Polish, Guatemalan, or Indonesian subset—go big. Who can give you inspiration for the challenges of your own life? Gudrid's story is a reminder that if you don't have someone admirable in your own genetic line, you can choose someone from your bigger clan of choice.

Too many of us are afflicted with a kind of historical and familial amnesia, especially in America where people tend to move frequently and often have tenuous connections with their extended network of relatives. We forget that we're embedded in a much larger set of stories, both individually and as a nation. Because of that, our own trials can seem even weightier. Lost your job? Dealing with a chronic illness? Try being a peasant in the Middle Ages, sister, or someone enslaved on a cotton plantation before the Civil War. Never forget that you come from a long line of people who had short, miserable lives (for that's what existence was like for most people for much of human history). Even a casual perusal of your family tree is likely to reveal scores of women who died in childbirth, parents who lost multiple young children to illness, and men who either died in war or were disabled for the rest of their lives. Not to mention the sorry state of dental care before the modern age.

By bringing these people consciously into your story, your perspective on your own life can change. Even if our own families are scattered or dysfunctional, ancestors can provide a sense of belonging in a world that often seems fragmented and isolating. Many cultures—from the Chinese and Mexican to the Nigerian—do a better job of honoring ancestors than ours. And first-generation college students, of which I'm one, often have a sense of what other people have sacrificed to enable us to spend our young adulthoods in classrooms rather than working full-time. Our success is partly because we stand on their shoulders.

I like to think of Gudrid as one of the ancestors who has my back, standing behind me when I'm in trouble, reminding me that I come from a long line of people who did audacious things. In counting her as my foremother, I also claim kinship with all those Scandinavians who consider her their ancestor. I'm a cousin many times removed, to be sure, but along with them I can still take pride in her courage and try to emulate her resourcefulness.

What's more, we might live our lives differently if we realize that *we* are potential ancestors and that our descendants might look to us for inspiration. That's true even if we don't have biological children. Often it's the aunts and uncles and other relatives and family friends, in fact, who play pivotal roles in young people's lives. They may devote themselves to careers in ways that parents can't, providing role models for professionalism and drive. They can do something as small as take the nieces and nephews out to the movies, or as large as leaving them an inheritance that makes it easier for them to begin a business, buy a house, or start a family.

This is what it means to perch on a branch of a family tree, gazing upwards, peering downwards, marveling at the tragedies and the triumphs we see all around us.

A VINLAND BETRAYAL

Every family has relatives no one wants to claim. In Leif and Gudrid's family, it was Freydis.

As my South Dakota mother-in-law once said about the bikers who attend the annual Harley Davidson rally in the Black Hills, "Most of them are very nice, even the ones who look tough. But of the ones who are scary, it's the women who are *really* scary."

That was certainly true of Freydis, Leif's half-sister who'd married a ne'er-do-well for his money. After Leif, Karlsefni, and Gudrid had returned from Vinland with tales of its bounty, the greedy Freydis hatched plans for her own expedition. She and her husband took command of a ship, and she approached two brothers with an offer that they could join them in another vessel. All proceeds from the expedition would be shared equally between the two parties.

Trouble began as soon as they arrived in Vinland when Freydis refused to allow the other boat's crew to stay in the longhouses built by Leif, demanding that they build their own dwellings instead. By the time the winter began, the two groups were so estranged that they kept to their separate houses instead of passing the long and tedious days of cold and darkness together.

Then Freydis orchestrated a much worse betrayal. Early one morning, unbeknownst to her husband, she went to the other camp and said she wanted to exchange her ship for theirs. The brothers agreed, even though their ship was the larger of the two. When Freydis went back to her own longhouse, however, she told a lie to her husband. "I went there to make an offer to buy their ship, but they struck and abused me," she said. "Unless you avenge this terrible dishonor, I will divorce you."

Her husband dutifully gathered his men and went to the opposing camp, where they tied the arms of its members and led them outside. Freydis insisted that they be killed, and so one by one they were murdered. When the men refused to touch the women of the group, Freydis asked for an ax and killed the five women herself.

Freydis was pleased with herself, but she knew she needed to keep the grisly story from spreading back home, so she made the members of her crew swear secrecy on pain of death. That spring, the expedition packed the two ships with trade goods they'd collected and sailed back to Greenland. It was said that their haul was the most lucrative of all the Vinland expeditions, giving much wealth to everyone involved. As in a Shakespearean tragedy, however, the evil didn't stay hidden. Eventually word of the betrayal that had happened in Vinland began to leak out. The other crew hadn't suffered natural deaths, as was reported, but were murdered.

When Leif heard the news, he thought it terrible, but he wasn't sure what to do. Think of it: here was a man who'd been a valued soldier to the king of Norway, who'd sailed the stormy Atlantic without a map, who founded a new colony in a foreign land, and who was renowned for his good sense and wisdom. But even he was flummoxed by his sister. "I'm not the one to deal my sister, Freydis, the punishment she deserves," he finally concluded, "but I predict that her descendants will not get on well in this world."

Leif was correct, as after that no one expected anything but evil from that branch of the family. Freydis fades from the story, leaving us with an image of her standing with ax in hand, the bodies of the five women at her feet. There are good reasons why no statues exist of Freydis, sister of Leif and sister-in-law of Gudrid.

So there you have it: proof that even the best of families has issues. Lucky Leif, the hero of Scandinavia, had both a father and a sister who were murderers. Though this family is separated from us by a thousand years, we can nod our heads in rueful sympathy. Good and evil are intertwined in every clan.

Gudrid's adventures, meanwhile, weren't over. Though the plans she and her husband had made to stay in Vinland failed, they still made a tidy profit from their time there. After leaving Vinland they traveled to Norway, where they were treated with great respect. They then went to Iceland, the land where both had been born. At first Karlsefni's mother was suspicious of Gudrid, whom she thought was beneath their social class, but the industrious and kind-hearted Gudrid won her over.

Gudrid would go on to give birth to another son, and following Karlsefni's death, she took over the running of the household, a place named Glaumbaer, the "Farm of Merry Noise." After her sons were adults, she traveled to Rome on pilgrimage, a journey nearly as epic as her trip to the New World. She likely took a ship to Denmark and from there walked to Rome, a distance of 1200 miles. After her return, she became a nun, though it's not clear what that involved in the context of the time, given how rudimentary the Christian church was in Iceland. It might have meant that she was devout and had taken her own, private vow not to marry again but instead devote her life to prayer.

I like to imagine her at the end of her life, thinking back on what she'd experienced. She'd made at least eight dangerous sea journeys, held her own around rough and uncultured men, delivered a baby in the wilderness, outlived two husbands, raised a couple of fine sons, and then set off on a pilgrimage that took her through foreign lands where she couldn't speak to the locals and was at the mercy of outlaws during a time when the great majority of women rarely traveled. She straddled the Old World and the New, as well as paganism and Christianity, with remarkable grace.

In her day she was called Gudrid Thorbjarnardottir, but in later centuries she was given a much more apt name: Gudrid the Far Traveler. Goodness knows, she'd earned it.

Costumed interpreters at L'Anse aux Meadows in Canada recreate life in the eleventh-century Vinland colony. (PHOTO BY BOB SESSIONS)

4

On the Edge of the World

-:❈:-

"Erickson?" repeated a guide at L'Anse aux Meadows when I told him my name. "You must be related to Leif. If we'd have known you were coming, we'd have had wine ready for you."

If there's any place where my last name has cachet, it's L'Anse aux Meadows in Canada. Once I started researching my ethnic roots, this place came up again and again. If I was going to find Leif anywhere, it would be here, in a place that's the only authenticated Viking site in North America.

For many years the Icelandic sagas, and the Vinland sagas in particular, were considered pretty worthless when it came to historical accuracy. Yes, they told interesting stories, and yes, there was probably some truth in them, but it was buried under so much exaggeration and literary flourishes that no one could separate the historical wheat from the fictional chaff. That changed in the spring of 1960 thanks to a pair of enterprising Norwegians who thought that the sagas' stories of Leif Eriksson's North-American explorations might be more accurate than most people believed. Years earlier, Helge Ingstad had left a legal career to become an author and explorer, setting off on adventures that included working as a trapper and hunter in the Canadian Arctic, living among the Apache in the United States, and serving in the underground resistance movement in Norway during World War II. His equally accomplished wife, Ann Stine Ingstad, was an archaeologist who shared his fascination for the Viking Age.

Armed with old maps and clues from the saga narratives, Helge Ingstad scoured the coasts of New England, Nova Scotia, Newfoundland, and Labrador by foot, airplane, and boat, searching for hints of Viking sites. In 1960 he came to the village of L'Anse aux Meadows on the northeastern tip of Newfoundland. There he asked the locals the same question he'd repeated many times before: Are there any strange land formations in the area? Why, yes, there are, said community elder George Decker. We have some Indian mounds. The kids like to play on them.

But to Ingstad, they didn't appear to be Indian mounds—instead they looked similar to the remains of Viking Age buildings he'd seen in Iceland. Beginning the next summer, Helge and Anne started excavating the mounds, finding artifacts left behind by the native peoples who'd occupied the site off and on for many centuries, as well as a few pieces of iron that were intriguing but inconclusive. Then in 1964 they hit the jackpot, though to the untrained eye this treasure looks pretty unremarkable: a small spindle whorl made of soapstone, a device that women of the Viking Age used to spin wool into thread. The whorl was definitive proof that the Vikings had indeed been there.

Subsequent excavations found more evidence. The structures that once stood near the village of L'Anse aux Meadows fit the pattern of eleventh-century buildings excavated in Iceland and Greenland. More artifacts were unearthed that were of Norse origin, including a bone needle, bronze pin, and glass bead. Archaeologists also found something that indicated that the Vikings had explored to the south: a butternut from a tree species found in New Brunswick but which has never grown as far north as Newfoundland. Finally, radiocarbon dating of various artifacts confirmed a time period of the eleventh century.

The Viking voyages to Vinland, it turns out, weren't fictional after all.

IN LEIF'S FOOTSTEPS

Even in an age of jet travel, it's not easy to get to L'Anse aux Meadows. First Bob and I flew from Chicago to Montreal, then to Halifax in Nova Scotia, and then to Deer Lake, Newfoundland. After spending the night, we set out the next morning in a rental car, winding our way northward along the aptly named Viking Trail, a 325-mile route lined with small fishing villages, dramatic fjords and mountains, and sweeping sea vistas framed by a rocky coastline. We passed through Gros Morne National Park, which has misty mountains and dense forests, and then drove past mile after mile of bogs, rocks, and scrubland with bushes that leaned landward because of the prevailing winds from the sea. The closer we got to L'Anse aux Meadows, the wilder the landscape became. We saw whales cavorting off the coast and icebergs headed south from the Arctic on the powerful Labrador Current. Occasionally, we passed moose that stood looking curiously at us from the edge of the forest.

As we traveled north, I thought about the long journey from Greenland made by Leif Eriksson, and later by Gudrid and her husband Thorfinn Karlsefni. They would have traveled on ships (called *knerrir* in Old Norse) that were wider, shorter, and deeper than the dragon-headed ships used for raiding. The journey across the North Atlantic likely took about two weeks, first heading across open sea and then south along the coast of Labrador. The weather was probably foul at times, with drenching rains, dense fog, and frigid winds—all the more miserable to endure because there was no place to take shelter below deck on Viking boats. For Leif, especially, it must at times have seemed like a foolish as well as dangerous journey. He was following the vague directions given by a merchant whose ship had blown off course while traveling between Iceland and Greenland. The man had spotted land to the west but hadn't investigated. While Leif could determine latitude by observing the angle of the sun, moon, and stars, he had no way of knowing longitude, which would have told him how far west he was traveling. And if the expedition got into trouble, there was no one who could rescue them.

It put into perspective the difficulties of my own trip to Newfoundland—a tiring day on airplanes, a nearly missed connection in Halifax, and a rental car with a confusing set of dashboard and audio controls. As the miles passed and the weather went from sun to rain and back to sun again, I appreciated the ease of modern travel—but a little part of me was also wistful when I thought of how it must have been, setting out for a new land in a boat powered by sails and hope.

After a good night's sleep in the seaside town of St. Anthony (where residents were excited about a couple of polar bears that had been seen outside of town), we drove the final few miles to our destination. Appropriately, the entrance to L'Anse aux Meadows is marked by the stylized representation of a Viking ship. From there a sidewalk leads to a visitor center set on a high spot overlooking the archaeological site. Standing on its deck, I savored the vista below me. Situated in a grassy expanse of meadow next to a shallow bay, L'Anse aux Meadows was lit by early morning sunshine. I could see a walking trail that led first to the area where the archaeological digs had been done and then to replicas of several Viking-era buildings. In the distance, icebergs floated in the brilliant blue waters of the bay—a view little different, no doubt, from that which the Vikings saw on summer mornings as they stepped outside to greet a new day.

My guide, serendipitously, turned out to be someone who knew the site better than almost anyone. Clayton Colbourne, a bearded, handsome man who looked to be in his seventies, introduced himself as a native of the area. "I grew up in the village of L'Anse aux Meadows and was one of the kids who played on the so-called Indian mounds," he said, pointing to the south. "My friends and I had a front-row seat for the excavations."

As we walked down the steps and across the boardwalk that led to the archaeological site, Clayton told of growing up almost completely isolated from the outside world and of how exciting it was when the Ingstads arrived. "All the locals thought they were crazy at first, but when they started discovering artifacts, we began to realize what an amazing site we had in our backyard," he said. "My family and I ended up becoming good friends with the Ingstads and the other archaeologists who worked here through the years."

Clayton told the story of the excavations with practiced ease. The Ingstads spent seven summers excavating at L'Anse aux Meadows, he said, and were followed by other archaeologists who laboriously sifted through the soil of L'Anse aux Meadows to search for clues about the Viking settlement. In 1968 Canada designated it a National Historic Site, and in 1978 it was named a UNESCO World Heritage Site, the first cultural site to be so honored.

"The buildings were likely constructed by Leif Eriksson and his men after their arrival in Newfoundland," said Clayton. "This settlement later became a base camp for expeditions that explored deeper into the region. At its height, about ninety people lived here. A small number of people wintered over, while the rest went back home to Greenland in the fall."

Our first stop along the trail was a small hillock that had once been a charcoal kiln used in the production of iron. Clayton explained that a substance called bog ore naturally forms here, a product of iron leaching out of the rocks and reacting chemically with the acidic waters of the bogs and streams. Before it can be used, it must be heated to a high temperature, which separates impurities from the iron. The Vikings used this iron in the production of nails to repair ships that had been damaged by the long voyage from Greenland.

Farther along the path, we came to an area with several sets of rounded walls of turf about a foot high. Clayton pointed out where three large halls once stood, each flanked by smaller huts. The largest was about 75 feet long and 10 feet wide, with the outlines of four rooms marked by raised mounds of grass.

"See that one over there?" he pointed. "That's where archae-ologists think that Leif Eriksson lived."

Leif's house was here, right here? I was surprised by how matter-of-fact Clayton was about the Leif Eriksson connec-tion. Before I arrived, I'd assumed there'd be hemming and hawing about the authenticity of the sagas, with hedging of bets and scholarly parsing. But Clayton presented this fact as casually as if Leif was a neighbor who used to live here, back in the day—which, of course, he was.

By this point, I'd done so much fanciful spinning of my connection to the explorer that when I was confronted with a direct link to him, I could barely contain myself. I knew I must look a little ridiculous, getting excited about what were, in fact, some ridges in the grass. But I didn't care. Bending down, I pressed my hand through the thick grass to reach the soil below. "Leif was here," I said in wonder.

I looked up at Clayton. "He was here?" I asked.

"Leif was here," he repeated, smiling.

And now I was here, too.

Still savoring the thrill of having stood in Leif's house, I next headed to the reconstructed buildings located near the archae-ological site. The largest of the three structures is a longhouse similar in size and layout to the house where Leif had lived. Made of a wooden frame covered with six-foot-thick sod and blending seamlessly with the earth around it, the place had a hobbit feel to it, as if Frodo were out for a walk but would be back shortly. Inside, I was surprised by how homey it was, with a flickering fire in the center of the room and sunlight stream-ing through openings in the roof. To the sides were platforms lined with furs for sleeping and lounging. The smell of cooking onions rose from a cauldron simmering on the fire, adding to the coziness of the scene.

"Welcome!" said a bearded man who was sitting near the fire mending a leather pouch. He was dressed in a gray, striped tunic over red trousers, a leather belt tied at his waist.

"I'm Lori Erickson, one of Leif Eriksson's relatives," I said, shamelessly name dropping. "A cousin several times removed."

The man's face lit up. "Leif!" he exclaimed. "A good man indeed! Of course, I have to say that because he owns these buildings. But he's a fine man. Well-liked. A good business-man. And mild-mannered, for a Viking."

Egil, it turns out, was a navigator on one of the ships that had brought the Norse to L'Anse aux Meadows. And a wily fel-low he was, too, clearly trying to get on my good side in hopes I'd put in a favorable word with my kinsman. Egil told me how smart he was to be able to guide ships across the North Atlantic and down the Labrador shore with its many coves and inlets. He offered to sing me a song, breaking into a dirgelike tune that made me realize that while the Vikings were rowdy, their music sometimes wasn't.

"Now, Egil, you mustn't monopolize our guest," said a woman who'd entered the room. "Introduce us, will you?"

"This is Anora, my wife," Egil said. "And a fine woman she is, too, at least when she obeys me."

Giving him a stern look, Anora took my arm. "Let's talk back here, where it's quieter," she said, leading me into an adjoining room where an upright loom was strung with fibers. A fire burned in the corner, casting a warm glow that left the other corners of the room in darkness.

"Do you weave?" she asked, seeing me peering closely at the loom.

"I don't know how to weave," I admitted.

"But how do you make your husband's clothing?" she asked in surprise. "And sails for your boat?"

"My husband doesn't have a boat," I said, deflecting atten-tion from my own lack of household skills. "He's too poor."

Anora tut-tutted, sympathetic to my plight. For the next half hour we traded stories, much to my delight—because if there's anything that sets a history nerd's heart beating faster, it's a conversation with someone who's a thousand years old. I learned about Anora's life, how she was one of a handful of women who lived at L'Anse aux Meadows and that she spent much of her time cooking, spinning, and weaving. She showed me her sleeping quarters at the other end of the longhouse, a room that had two box-shaped closet beds with curtains to keep the warmth of body heat inside.

Our conversation gave me a vivid sense of the challenges of Gudrid's life here. As the chieftain's wife, she would have directed the many tasks needed to keep the settlement fed and clothed. Days filled with household chores—and later caring for her baby son—must have kept her busy from morning until night. By the time she crawled into that bedstead, she would have been tired indeed.

Outside the longhouse, I was introduced to another member of the community, a thrall named Wolfric. Remembering that *thrall* was another word for slave, I was eager to talk to him, curious about how L'Anse aux Meadows would interpret this aspect of Norse society. Dressed in a brown tunic, he didn't appear that different from the other Vikings on site. But sitting next to him on a bench, I was conscious of the fact that in real life, a thrall wouldn't have had the leisure to visit at length with a passing stranger.

Once Wolfric sensed my keen interest in the topic of slavery, he switched out of character in order to give me a more complete view of the practice. "People sometimes tell me how much they'd like to go back in time and be a Viking," he began. "I tell them, 'Not me, not for a minute. I'm a slave, remember?'" He explained that at L'Anse aux Meadows, the social structure had consisted of the expedition leader and his wife at the top, skilled laborers and craftsmen below them, and slaves at the bottom. While the sagas indicate that there were thralls in Vinland, the exact number isn't known.

"How did people become slaves?" I asked.

"A variety of ways," he said. "Sometimes they were taken on raids, and sometimes people voluntarily became thralls because they couldn't support themselves. Others were enslaved after committing a crime or because they couldn't pay their debts. The children of slaves became slaves themselves. We know that during this era in Norway, about 20 to 30 percent of the population were in bondage."

Thralls did the grunt work of Norse life—duties that included spreading manure on fields, tending animals, clearing land, digging peat, building houses, grinding flour, and milking. They typically lived side by side with their owners, though the hair of the men was kept short so that they could be easily identified as slaves.

Wolfric said that slavery in the Viking world was a more fluid category than we might assume. Thralls could conduct business on their own and could own their own home and animals. They could earn their freedom through hard work, though it often took several generations before their family achieved full respectability in Norse society. As he spoke, I remembered that one of the reasons that Gudrid's mother-in-law didn't approve of her was probably because her grandmother had been a slave. Still, within three generations Gudrid's family had gone from bondage to wealth—an indication of the ways in which Viking slavery was less harsh than in many other societies.

And then I recalled the story of the slave girl sacrificed at the chieftain's funeral. Not all women in the Viking Age were as fortunate as Gudrid.

AN ISOLATED OUTPOST

The visitor center rounded out my introduction to life at L'Anse aux Meadows. Exhibits there described how it was an unusual Norse settlement in a number of ways. While they might have had a small number of animals to provide meat, milk, cheese, and butter, the Vikings didn't farm in Newfoundland. Instead it was a place for boat repairs—sail mending, carpentry, iron smelting, and smithing—and a base for further expeditions into the larger region. Their largest export product was probably wood, a precious commodity in treeless Greenland, but they also dealt in furs and wine made from grapes harvested in lands to the south. The trips back and forth to Greenland were made between June and September, a short window of time when the weather was best (though in Newfoundland, the weather can turn wintry in any month).

Having seen the replica buildings up close, I had a greater appreciation for the work involved in their construction. One of the reasons that archaeologists think L'Anse aux Meadows was the major Viking settlement in Vinland, in fact, was the sheer effort it took to build it. A crew of sixty men likely labored for about two months to construct the buildings. As the explorers traveled south from L'Anse aux Meadows, they certainly had temporary encampments, but given the amount of work and materials that went into the structures here, it's unlikely there was more than one settlement of this size.

I paused in front of a map showing the sailing routes taken by the Norse across the North Atlantic. The shore of Labrador is deeply indented with bays and inlets, which added many miles to their journeys because Viking sailors tried to stay in sight of land as much as possible for safety reasons. I could see how the location of L'Anse aux Meadows made practical sense. It sits near the entrance to the St. Lawrence Seaway, giving easy access to the interior of the continent. The landscape of the region must have seemed familiar to Greenlanders—the rocky shores, the windswept expanses, the boggy wetlands. And the water level was higher during that period, so boats could have easily docked in the bay next to the settlement.

One of the major questions relating to the Norse expeditions in North America concerns the name Vinland, which Leif Eriksson gave to his colony. It likely comes from *vin*, meaning wine, a reference to the drink made from the grapes that the explorers found in abundance. The problem is that grapes have never grown in Newfoundland, even during a warmer period in its climate. In response, most scholars say that it's best to think of Vinland as an entire region rather than one location. L'Anse aux Meadows probably marked the northernmost point of Vinland, an area that extended south into Nova Scotia and New Brunswick, where wild grapes flourished.

Birgitta Wallace, who succeeded the Ingstads as the chief archaeologist at L'Anse aux Meadows, has a theory for why Leif chose to name the territory Vinland. In Norse society, the mark of a very wealthy man was being able to offer wine to his guests, for grapes didn't grow in Norway and wine had to be imported. Coming as he did from a family of humble origins, Leif likely took great pride in his Vinland wines, which increased his social status as well as fattened his coffers.

According to the sagas, the Norse launched four expeditions to Vinland. The first was led by Leif; the second, by his brother Thorvald; and the third, by Karlsefni and Gudrid. The fourth was the ill-fated expedition led by the treacherous Freydis. Mounting an expedition was an expensive proposition, but the potential rewards were also great. The crew shared in the profits (except the slaves, of course), which was an added incentive for skilled laborers to join the group.

While archaeological evidence indicates that L'Anse aux Meadows was occupied by indigenous peoples before and after the Norse settlement, during the period the Vikings were here, it was uninhabited, which was probably another reason why this spot was chosen. But the Norse had multiple interactions with the natives (the Skraelings) when they visited their camp and on their own travels through the region. In Labrador and Newfoundland, these people may have been the ancestors of the Innu and Beothuk; farther south, the Mi'kmaq. The encounters were sometimes cordial and at other times deadly. According to the sagas, Leif's brother, the leader of the second expedition, was killed in a skirmish that also left nearly a dozen of the Skraelings dead.

Then, after about ten years of occupation, the Norse left. There were growing conflicts with the Skraelings, and the trip back to Greenland was too long to be economically profitable. It was 1,350 nautical miles from L'Anse aux Meadows to the settlement of Brattahlid in Greenland—more than 300 miles longer than from L'Anse aux Meadows to the major Viking port of Bergen, Norway. The journey was riskier, too, especially since it involved traveling through the icebergs that float south on the Labrador Current.

As I toured the L'Anse aux Meadows visitor center, I was surprised by how few artifacts remain from the Norse settlement. When the Vikings returned to Greenland, they took most of their goods with them, leaving behind some broken items and a handful of objects probably left by accident, an indication that their retreat was orderly and well planned. The buildings were burned to the ground, almost certainly by the Vikings themselves, because they were too valuable a resource to leave for others to use.

I peered at the Norse artifacts on display, which included iron rivets and nails, slag left over from smelting, part of a knitting needle made of bone, and a pin used to fasten a cloak. Most intriguing of all was the spindle whorl made of soapstone, the one that had generated such excitement when it was found by the Ingstads. It was the one artifact I most wanted to see at L'Anse aux Meadows, the lure that made me travel 2,500 miles from my home.

The spindle whorl was even smaller than I'd expected, just a donut-shaped piece of stone about an inch-and-a-half in diameter. I knew that only a few women had lived in the Vinland settlement, and it was well within the realm of possibility that Gudrid herself had used it. I spent a long time staring at it through the glass, willing it to speak to me, but it remained silent, a mute witness to a life that I can enter only in my imagination.

AT HOME WITH THE VIKINGS

L'Anse aux Meadows isn't the only Viking settlement in this corner of the world, as I learned the next day when I visited a site called Norstead just across the road. Norstead is a twin attraction to the World Heritage Site, a re-creation of a Viking era settlement in Iceland. Like L'Anse aux Meadows, it's situated on the shore of a peaceful bay, with a collection of sod-and-frame buildings arrayed on shore. But while the archaeological site focuses on the particularities of the Vinland expedition, Norstead portrays a more general picture of life in the era.

I proved equally fortunate in my guide at Norstead as I had at L'Anse aux Meadows. In fact, when I was introduced to her, I squealed at a volume that startled us both.

"You're Gudrid?! I can't believe it," I exclaimed. Then I enveloped her in a hug, which she returned with good-natured warmth.

It turned out, however, that Gudrid at Norstead isn't quite the Gudrid of the Vinland sagas. Known outside of work hours as Denecka Burden, she's the director of Norstead, having worked her way up to that position from being a part-time interpreter. When she heard about my fascination for Gudrid the Far Traveler, she laughed. "Hardly anyone knows about Gudrid the Far Traveler when they come here," she said. "And I'm not exactly Gudrid, but rather a high-status woman of the time period. But Gudrid might well have worn something like this." She pointed out details of her dress that indicated she was at the top of the social ladder: a red-dyed tunic edged with embroidery, a fur-trimmed jacket, and imported beads on her necklace. The outfit was attractive, even by modern standards.

Next Gudrid helped me into my own Norse attire: first a blue dress made of linen, then a brown apron fastened at the shoulders with two large metal brooches. "May I have a sword, too?" I asked, eying a weapon I'd spied at the bottom of the clothes box.

"Well, there were women warriors, but you won't need a weapon for your visit here," said Gudrid.

Instead, I needed household skills. First I helped cook a pot of stew over an open fire in the longhouse, then I tried my hand at Norse knitting, which used a single needle instead of two. I was doing pretty well at pretending to be a Norse housewife until I got to drop spinning, which uses a spindle whorl like I'd seen in the visitor center. The interpreter explained that the making of cloth was an essential skill for women, since it was often the only saleable commodity a farm produced. I watched as she took a clump of wool, pulled some fibers away from it, formed them into a string, and then swung a spindle whorl in circles to twist the fiber to make it stronger.

It looked easy when her nimble fingers did the process, but when I tried it, the thread kept breaking, the whorl spun crazily, and the resulting yarn was bumpy and uneven. Despite my Scandinavian lineage, I was clearly a very sorry excuse for a Viking woman.

"This is definitely harder than it looks," I said in frustration.

"Don't worry, my dear," said the motherly interpreter. "Women like you can always do the cooking."

I felt like telling her I could read and write—a rarity for anyone in the period, especially women—but then realized those skills wouldn't have been very useful on a Viking Age farm either. In this era, women were most prized for their household expertise, childbearing and rearing, and ability to manage a farm when their husbands were absent. In the words of Birgitta Wallace, "One gets the impression from the sagas that strength and fearlessness [in women] were more admired than delicacy."

With relief I handed the wool back to the interpreter and then headed to the next building. There, thankfully, all I had to do was be awestruck, because inside was a *knarr*, a replica of the type of boat that scholars think the Norse sailed to Newfoundland. Despite its lack of dragon heads, it was an impressive vessel, about fifty feet long, with overlapping planks held together by iron rivets. An interpreter dressed in the simple tunic and cloak of a laborer invited me to climb a ladder so that I could see its deck. Wide and open, it would have had a single mast and sail when out to sea.

"This type of boat held about thirty people," the guide explained. "The crew also brought along all the supplies needed for the new colony. They probably had livestock, too, so it was pretty crowded."

"Lots of manure, no doubt," I said, imagining just how much poop a few cows and sheep could create over a couple of weeks.

"They would have just pushed it off the deck into the sea," he said. "But even so, it certainly wasn't a pleasure cruise."

Viewed up close, the boat was large and impressive, but I knew it must have seemed small indeed when its passengers were being tossed about by the rough waters of the North Atlantic. I remembered, too, that many Viking boats never reached their destinations. On Erik the Red's voyage from Iceland to Greenland, for example, the one where he led a group of people to populate his new colony, eleven out of twenty-five ships were lost en route. Drop spinning was among the least difficult of the many challenges faced by the Norse.

My last stop at Norstead was its small church, which is modeled after the remains of a church excavated in Greenland that is said to have been built by Leif Eriksson for his mother. No grand house of worship for the newly converted Vikings of this era—instead the building's grass-covered walls and roof make it look more like a root cellar than a church.

Stepping inside, I saw rough-hewn wooden benches lining its walls and a simple altar. The church's plainness reminded me that while basilicas, cathedrals, and other impressive religious landmarks hog the ecclesiastical limelight, modest churches like this one are much more common in Christianity, especially in past centuries. For families who stayed rooted in the same area for generations, these buildings were the site of their baptisms, weddings, and funerals, of Christmases and Easters and all the services in between. When we trace the lives of our ancestors, it's easy to forget how tied many of them were to particular places of worship. Those ties may seem inconsequential when viewed from the perspective of today, but to those who prayed in these humble buildings, they were as much home as the houses in which they lived.

The next day, I returned to L'Anse aux Meadows, eager to have the chance to reflect more deeply on all that I'd learned. Once again, the weather was sunny and warm—a rarity in Newfoundland in any season or era. This time I chose to be by myself, walking along the beach and then across the headland that overlooked L'Anse aux Meadows, finally finding a spot to sit near the archaeological site. Even with several dozen tourists wandering around, it was peaceful, with seagulls cawing and wheeling overhead. In the bay I could see an island void of any sign of human life and icebergs bobbing in the water like children's bath toys.

I thought again about Gudrid's experiences in Vinland. She probably gave birth to her son in the same house where Leif once lived, since she and Karlsefni were leaders of their expedition. I imagined her giving birth there, with two or three other women to help with labor and delivery, and then raising her child in the isolated community. The summers must have been incredibly busy; the winters less so, with their short days and long nights. Lots of time for spinning and weaving of cloth, no doubt. Given Gudrid's formidable talents, I bet she was good at both.

I knew a great deal about Gudrid yet at the same time tantalizingly little. I kept thinking of the spindle whorl, that little item she might have used as she sat by the fire. The lives of most Viking women were small and circumscribed, bounded by hearth and family, yet this woman hadn't been content with all that the whorl symbolized. Instead, she'd sailed from Iceland to Greenland to Newfoundland, then back again to Iceland and Norway. Later in life, she took another epic journey when she went on pilgrimage to Rome.

I thought of all she likely experienced on that trip: the bustling cities of central Europe, the chatter of unfamiliar languages, impressive buildings of stone rather than wood, markets selling luxury goods she'd never seen before, meals with rich flavors unlike the simple cuisine of the North. And the Alps— what did she think of those huge mountains? And what were her impressions of Rome, that city filled with churches and cathedrals grander than any building she'd seen before? Did she make friends along the way? She probably did, since she was a woman who knew how to behave around strangers.

Certainly when Gudrid was old, after her journeys had finally ended, she had a wealth of memories to turn over in her mind, there at the Farm of Merry Noise. I wondered how often she thought about her time in Vinland.

As for me, however, my travels would continue. With a sigh, I stood up, because it was my own turn to leave L'Anse aux Meadows.

In the Norse world, the destiny of humans and gods was controlled by supernatural beings known as the Norns. (ILLUSTRATION BY CHARLES EDWARD BROCK)

5

Back to the Future

–◦✳◦–

"I think it might have been a mistake to name our cat Loki,"
I told Bob, closing the book of Norse mythology I was reading. Several years ago, it had seemed like a good idea to name
our two new cats after a Norse god and goddess, a nod to
my ethnic heritage and to the book I was beginning to write.
Freya was easy—she was the goddess of love who traveled
in a chariot drawn by cats. Loki was a natural choice, too,
because he was a trickster deity, playful and charming, just
like the little black-and-white kitten we'd gotten from an animal shelter.

However, the more I learned about the Norse pantheon, the
more I thought that Loki might have been an unwise choice.
He was a trickster, yes, but those tricks were often cruel. Capri-
cious, cunning, and witty, he was an Oscar-Wilde-sort-of-god
with a serious dark side. He sometimes saved his fellow deities
from trouble, but more often he sowed discord. His final act of
betrayal resulted in Ragnarök, the Twilight (sometimes translated as Doom) of the Gods, when the world was engulfed in
flames and almost all the gods were destroyed. It all made me
look at our Loki with a wary eye, watching for signs that he

might turn on us, and not just by sharpening his claws on the downstairs couch when we weren't around.

My forays into Norse mythology were actually a return journey, for one of my favorite childhood books was Ingri and Edgar Parin D'Aulaire's *Norse Gods and Giants*, a lavishly illustrated tome full of stories of Thor, Odin, Loki, Freya, and their divine kindred. I was fascinated by how different these tales were from the Bible stories I heard in our Lutheran church in rural Iowa. Many of the biblical narratives were also full of drama, from a flood that destroyed everything on earth except for the creatures in Noah's ark to the shepherd boy David slaying the giant Goliath. But the Norse world was bizarre on an entirely different scale, with magic rings, giant serpents, shining elves who flew on gossamer wings, and gnomes who mined precious metals deep underground. This world had three beings, called the Norns, who controlled human destiny like the Fates in Greek mythology, plus so many gods, goddesses, and other supernatural beings that I couldn't keep them all straight. It surprised me that my Norwegian ancestors once had a set of gods much rowdier than the Christian Trinity, and when I sang the familiar hymn about what a friend we have in Jesus, I couldn't help but think that Thor might be a better choice when things got difficult.

Memories of that childhood book came back as I returned to the Norse myths as an adult. I snuggled under a blanket in the window seat of my bedroom as the first snowfall of winter fell outside, a tall stack of library books piled on the table next to me. I opened the top one, and it took just a few pages for me to be immersed in the gods' dramas and battles once again, the white flakes drifting down outside a fitting backdrop to these tales set in the frigid north.

Curiously, after a few minutes of reading, my other cat jumped up and settled into my lap: Freya, a reserved feline who'd never voluntarily come into my lap before. But as I was reading about her namesake, she appeared out of nowhere, nestled into my lap, and started to purr. I looked into her emerald green eyes, intrigued by what looked suspiciously like amusement on her face.

Because the Vikings had an oral culture, rather than a written one, figuring out what they believed isn't easy. What we do know comes from observations by outsiders, who undoubtedly misinterpreted at least some of what they saw (think how clueless we'd be if we were transported into a remote jungle and had to figure out what native tribes were doing in their ceremonies). We also have stories written by Christians who lived centuries after the Viking Age ended, people who tried to record the oral traditions of pagan Norse culture but who often wanted to emphasize their faith's superiority over the heathen ways of the wild Norse.

One man in particular deserves our thanks: the thirteenth-century Icelandic chieftain Snorri Sturluson (and let me just add that I think it's a terrible shame that so few parents today name their children Snorri). At one time he was the wealthiest man in Iceland, a wheeler-dealer of prodigious energy. Unscrupulous and conniving, he pushed his seven children into unhappy marriages to increase his own status. In the end he'd double-crossed too many people and died at the hands of a mob that included two of his former sons-in-law.

Despite his personal limitations, Snorri did us a tremendous favor by compiling the stories of his homeland into the *Prose Edda*. Along with the *Poetic Edda*, a collection of anonymous poems recorded around the same time, it's our primary source for Norse mythology. Snorri wanted to preserve the stories that were in danger of disappearing and also to help poets who were losing the ability to understand kenning, a common literary device in Icelandic verse. The term refers to the practice of calling a noun by a code phrase. Gold, for example, could be referred to as Sif's hair, a reference to a story in which Loki cut off the goddess Sif's locks and had to commission a dwarf to make a gold wig for her. Mistletoe was known as Baldur's bane because it was the cause of his death (all plants and animals on earth had pledged to his mother Frigg that they wouldn't harm him, except for the lowly mistletoe). Icelandic poetry of the day was full of kenning, but as their origin stories died out, these references became more and more obscure.

Birthed in the harsh landscape of Scandinavia, the tales have a surreal quality to them, full of shape-shifting, reversals of fortune, revenge, deceit, and sly humor, all overshadowed by the knowledge that the entire world is going to come to a most unpleasant end in an apocalypse known as Ragnarök. The Norse gods are both immortal and mortal—just one of the many paradoxes of this mythology.

These dramas took place in a cosmos of nine worlds linked by an enormous tree named Yggdrasil. The gods who lived in its upper branches belonged to two families, the Aesir, powerful and warlike, and the Vanir, who were more interested in fertility (think babies, good fishing, and bounteous harvests). At one point the two sets of gods went to war against each other and then agreed in a truce that they would exchange gods. Freya, a divine party girl with a love for all sensual and material pleasures, was among the three Vanir who went to live in the Norse Olympia known as Asgard. The most sought-after real estate in the realm of the gods was Valhalla, where dead warriors were carried from the battlefield by Odin's handmaidens, who were known as Valkyries. No resting on billowy clouds for these men: instead they fought all day, feasted at night, and then got up the next morning to do it all again.

Other worlds included Jotunheim, the land of the giants, and the subterranean realm of Nidavellir, where the dwarves mined precious metals that they shaped into magical objects. Humans dwelled in Midgard, which was encircled by a giant serpent and connected by a rainbow bridge to Asgard. Below Yggrasil was the realm of the underworld, where the goddess Hel ruled over those not fortunate enough to have died in battle. It wasn't a place of torment and suffering like the Christian hell, but it certainly wasn't the whoop-it-up paradise of Valhalla either.

Most of the Viking gods were as fierce as the Vikings them-selves. Take red-bearded Thor, for example, who was quick to anger but also brave and loyal. He rode around heaven in a chariot pulled by two goats named Teeth-gnasher and Teeth-barer. If he was short on food, he could eat them for dinner, and the next morning—assuming he'd carefully saved all their bones and skin—they were reborn and could serve him another day.

Thor's most prized possessions were his hammer, a pair of iron gloves that he needed to wield it, and a belt that doubled his already prodigious strength. He was the god of thunder (a sound made when his chariot wheels rolled across heaven) and lightning (which sparked from his hammer and from the hooves of his goats as they trotted). Despite being a little dim-witted, he frequently defended the gods in conflicts with the Frost Giants and other creatures that wished to do them harm.

Of all the divine pantheon, Thor was the most popular with the common people. Throughout Scandinavia, sacri-fices were made to him in times of disease or famine, and many people wore a small medallion of his hammer around their necks. He was so popular that in the *Icelandic Book of Settlements*, a history of the early years of the island, a full one-quarter of the names include some cognate of Thor (and many years later in Iowa, my great-grandparents gave my grandfather the middle name of Thorvald, showing that the tradition continued in America).

Less popular, but at the top of everyone's list of whom not to offend, was Odin, the father of the gods. He was such a passionate seeker of knowledge that he plucked out his own eye in exchange for the chance to drink from a magical well of wisdom. He also hung himself upside down for nine days and nights on Yggrasil in exchange for the ability to read runes, the Norse form of writing that had magical properties. A raven named Thought and another named Memory were his com-panions, birds that he sent out into the world each day to gather news. He rode an eight-legged horse, could speak to the dead, and was a master of poetry and sorcery. He was typically pictured as an old man with a gray beard and a hat that hid much of his face (picture Gandalf here, for J. R. R. Tolkien later incorporated elements of Odin into his own wizard).

The color and drama of the Norse world greatly appealed to me, but at the same time I had to acknowledge that this branch of my spiritual clan had its faults: bitter feuds, broken marriages, wanton promiscuity, domestic abuse, and criminal behavior ranging from theft and kidnapping to murder. Not to mention some pretty serious medical issues. Divine pregnancies could result in the birth of children who were serpents or wolves (imagine what it would be like to have one of these show up on a pregnancy ultrasound). And poor Loki's daughter Hel, who ruled the underworld, was a maiden on one side of her body and a corpse on the other. I was grateful, frankly, not to share a genetic link with them.

Although it's been many centuries since my relatives worshiped this crew, as I immersed myself in their stories I felt something stirring deep within, a pleasurable flicker of what felt almost like an ancestral memory. The realization included some trepidation, however, because I suspected that once the Norse gods are awakened, pretty much anything can happen.

SNORRI'S CHILDREN

It's difficult to read Snorri Sturluson's *Prose Edda* without thinking, "Hey, this guy stole a bunch of material from *The Lord of the Rings*." The reason, of course, is that J. R. R. Tolkien fell under the spell of Norse mythology just as Snorri had done centuries before. As a teenager Tolkien taught himself Old Norse in order to read Icelandic literature in the original, and during his tenure as a professor of Anglo-Saxon at the University of Oxford, he championed the brilliance of the Norse myths and Icelandic sagas to his students and colleagues. Literary critic Guy Davenport writes, "Tolkien, who could speak Elvish and West Saxon, gave up the study of Greek because it was so orderly, logical, and articulate. He turned to the languages of the European North that smelled of bogs and mist."

To entertain his children, Tolkien began writing stories that drew heavily on the literature of the North that so captivated him. Eventually a draft of *The Hobbit* caught the attention of a publishing house, which printed it in 1937. The much longer and more complex *The Lord of the Rings* trilogy followed in 1954–55. The phenomenal popularity of Tolkien's work launched a fascination for fantasy that continues to this day, influencing writers that include C. S. Lewis, Anne McCaffrey, Neil Gaiman, Douglas Adams, Lloyd Alexander, Terry Brooks, J. K. Rowling, and Stephen King. Moreover, all the books, movies, graphic novels, and games filled with wizards, elves, trolls, gods, dragons, warriors, and giants owe their existence in part to the portly, morally compromised Snorri laboring at a table in his home in Iceland, recording the stories of his people as the Northern Lights swirled above him. Without Snorri, we wouldn't have Dungeons and Dragons, World of Warcraft, George R. R. Martin's *Game of Thrones,* or Marvel's Thor.

This familiarity, however, may lead us to believe that we know Norse religious beliefs better than we actually do. Much of their worldview is a mystery to us, in part because they had no central dogma or organized religious hierarchy but instead beliefs, practices, and stories that varied depending on the region. They shared their world with many types of supernatural beings, some visible and some not, from elves and dwarves to spirits associated with caves, mountains, and bodies of water. They mainly worshiped outdoors in sacred groves and on holy mountains, but they also had home altars and temples. Religious rituals often included offerings of valuable objects such as weapons, jewelry, food, and sacrificed animals. Blood, which was considered sacred and powerful, would be sprinkled on the statues of gods, on the participants in ceremonies, and on the walls of shrines. And their funerals were big-deal events, with the Norse either burying or burning their dead with items they would need in the next life (think of that Viking funeral with the sacrificed slave girl).

One of the most vivid descriptions of Norse religion comes from Adam of Bremen, an eleventh-century Christian from Germany who compiled reports from eyewitnesses who'd visited the great temple at Uppsala, Sweden. He writes that inside the large wooden hall were statues of Thor, Odin, and Frey (the brother of Freya). People made sacrifices to Thor in times of plague or famine, to Odin for victory in war, and to Frey for happiness in marriage.

Every nine years a nine-day ceremony was held that included an extravaganza of sacrifices. "Of every living creature they offer nine head, and with the blood of those it is the custom to placate the gods, but the bodies are hanged in a grove which is near the temple; so holy is that grove to the heathens that each tree in it is presumed to be divine by reason of the victim's death and putrefaction. There also dogs and horses hang along with men. One of the Christians told me that he had seen seventy-two bodies of various kinds hanging there." Adam of Bremen's description of the limp bodies of dogs, horses, and men hanging from the trees is a reminder that at least some of the Norse took their religion very seriously indeed.

ANCESTRAL BELIEFS

Genealogy buffs are interested in nearly everything about their dead relatives—where they were born and when they got married, what their occupation was, and how and when they died. From official records and historical research we can get a pretty good idea of their living conditions, what they ate, and what their work involved, be it farming or running a grist mill or blacksmithing. With some imagination, we can put ourselves in the shoes of a fishmonger in sixteenth-century London or a civil servant in eighteenth-century China.

However, the religious beliefs of our kin are much more of a mystery, for the interior workings of the human heart are invisible even to someone sitting in a chair next to us. If your great-grandmother was Jewish, you don't know if she actually believed the words she prayed or was mostly going through the motions. Your Utah ancestors might have been Mormons in good standing or Jack Mormons (who are kinda-sorta members of the faith but not when it comes to the hard parts, like tithing). When your forefather left Holland on an immigrant boat, maybe he heaved a sigh of relief that he'd never have to endure another sermon by a long-winded minister, or perhaps his heart ached at the thought of never again worshiping God in his family's ancestral church. Even if the names of our relatives are recorded in parish registries, even if we know they were confirmed or bar mitzvahed or married in a religious ceremony, we can't be entirely sure of their beliefs unless we find a diary that says the equivalent of either "I love Jesus with all my heart" or "I don't believe any of this stuff."

That said, much of what we know about our ancestors comes because of their affiliation with an organized religion. In Christianity, for example, baptism records are considered among the most reliable of sources because they were independent corroborations of a birth by someone who was at least minimally educated. Records of ceremonies in Judaism, Islam, and other religions are also valued highly. Members of the Church of Jesus Christ of Latter-day Saints, of course, set the gold standard for religious genealogy, recording the data of millions of people. Even if you're not a believer in any of these religions, you can be grateful for the information they've saved over the centuries.

It's also true that religions have genealogies just as individuals do. Judaism can be thought of as the parent of both Christianity and Islam, and a diagram showing the multitude of Christian denominations bears a resemblance to the family tree of a particularly hot-tempered clan who got divorced at the drop of a hat, though it's generally over theology and not sex (in the case of the Anglicans and Henry VIII, it's both). If you could sample the spiritual DNA of most people of faith, in short, the test would show traces of a variety of belief systems.

But why should we concern ourselves with the religious beliefs of our ancestors at all, especially if we're thoroughly secular in our own worldviews? One reason is that for much

of human history, spiritual beliefs were among the most powerful forces shaping people's lives. They influenced how people treated one another and structured their days, how they
dealt with difficulties and tragedies, and how they approached
death. Through the centuries, religion has inspired art and
music, provided the basis for legal codes, launched wars and
brokered truces, and inspired both the best and the worst in
our species. An atheist viewpoint, it turns out, is an anomaly
in world history.

I think of Gudrid the Far Traveler, who during her lifetime
saw the transition from a pagan world to a Christian one. What
did she believe would happen to her after she died? When people she loved were seriously ill, did she sneak in a prayer to a
pagan god, just in case? Part of the reason that she so fascinates
me, I realize, is that I also live in a time of shifting religious traditions. I, too, sometimes feel like I'm standing on the border
between realms, in my case between Christianity and a culture
where fewer and fewer people take religion seriously.

And the more I learned about the world of the Norse, the
more the question nagged at me: What in the world happened to them? Why did the Scandinavians exchange their
rowdy set of deities for Christianity and then for a particularly buttoned-down version of Lutheranism? Why did they
eventually become even more Lutheran than the Germans?
And is there any of that Norse pagan passion still left in Scandinavia, or in those of us who claim descent from that part
of the world?

Actually, there are many people who still draw inspiration
from Norse spiritual traditions, according to Kari Tauring, a
woman from Minneapolis who describes herself as a Nordic
Roots author, educator, and performer.

I was introduced to Kari's work when a friend suggested
I check out her materials on the Internet. In YouTube videos, books, workshops, and blog posts, Kari describes a
spiritual path called Völva Stav, which she has developed

based on traditions from pre-Christian Scandinavia. The practice combines rituals, songs, and stories from the past with original material drawn from her training as a musician, dancer, and scholar.

Her videos in particular captured my interest. I watched in growing fascination as a woman with a bright smile and expressive features gave an overview of Norse spiritual beliefs and then reinterpreted them for the modern age. She described the staff-carrying women (known in Old Norse as *völva*) who performed ceremonies and helped transmit cultural knowledge. Often living independently, they kept themselves separate from the larger society so that they could provide impartial, wise counsel. As she spoke, I was reminded of the wandering seeress who'd prophesied the future to Gudrid during that cold winter in Iceland described in *The Saga of Erik the Red*. Thorbjorg had been a *völva*, I now realized, remembering the staff she'd carried and how much respect she was accorded by the desperate people who sought her counsel.

Kari's videos gave a succinct description of two concepts I'd run across in my reading but hadn't fully understood. The first was *wyrd*, an Old Norse word that's sometimes translated as fate or destiny. The Vikings believed that all of life was governed by fate. "Fate occupied roughly the same position in the Norse worldview that the laws of science do in the modern world; it provided an unseen guiding principle that determined how events in the world would unfold, and could explain them after they occurred," writes Daniel McCoy in *The Viking Spirit: An Introduction to Norse Mythology and Religion*. "Questioning the reality and omnipotence of fate would have been laughable and almost unthinkable."

Öorlog might be thought of as a subset of *wyrd*, though it's difficult to come up with a comprehensive definition of it, both because it's a complex idea and because its original meaning is obscured by the passage of many centuries. If you think of it as a word cloud, one of those computer-generated images in which the size of each word indicates its importance, the most prominent terms for *öorlog* would be *primal law, fate, destiny,* and *karma,* but other terms would be floating around in the mix too, including *ancestors, past, inheritance,* and *primal layers.* However it's defined, the Norse believed that the three supernatural beings known as the Norns determined a baby's *öorlog* when it's born, and that even the gods were governed by *öorlog.*

It wasn't until I saw one of Kari's videos that the meaning of the word clicked into place for me. She spoke of the Norns as representing three aspects of life: Urd rules the past; Verdandi governs the present; and Skurd oversees necessity. Then she picked up a drop spindle, one similar to the ones used by reenactors at the Viking village of Norstead in Newfoundland. Holding the wooden implement in one hand and a clump of unspun wool in the other, she explained that the string already spun on the bobbin represents the *öorlog* you've received from your ancestors. The present is where your fingers come together at the point where the thread meets the unspun wool. And the third Norn, necessity, relates to the decisions you make as you spin that wool into thread. If you need a pair of socks, the yarn should be thick and warm, while a garment might need a finer thread. We spin the type of thread that's needed for our lives. The homely metaphor, so deeply Scandinavian, helped explain the metaphysical concept that had eluded me before.

Most of all, I was intrigued by how this woman was bringing the ancient Norse stories to life. This wasn't just mythology—she was talking about a living spiritual tradition, one that I could explore myself.

Within a week, a set of Norse runes I'd purchased through Kari Tauring's website arrived in the mail. I arranged them on a table before me, twenty-four round pieces of light-colored wood about an inch in diameter, each bearing a unique design of angular, primitive-looking marks. I had no idea what the designs meant, but that didn't matter. I knew my ancestors had used them a thousand years ago, and that was enough to get me started. Kari Tauring wasn't the only Scandinavian American who could make the past her own.

THE GIFT OF THE RUNES

The first written mention of the Norse runes comes from the first-century Roman historian Tacitus, who wrote that the tribes of the North made marks on twigs and threw them on a white cloth to divine messages from their gods. Our main sources for the individual meanings of the runes are three poems dating from the early medieval age but drawing on older, oral traditions. When interest in the runes was revived during the nineteenth century, people turned to these poems to try to re-create rune divination for a contemporary audience. Most used a set of runes that came to be known as the Elder Futhark. *Elder* refers to the fact that it is the oldest of several sets of runes that existed through the centuries, and *Futhark* is a combination of the sounds of its first six letters (much like *alphabet* is a combination of *alpha* and *beta*, the first two letters of the Greek alphabet).

The origin story of the runes, the one in which Odin hung himself on the world tree Yggdrasil for nine days and nights, reinforced their association with magic and emphasized the fact that these were powerful tools to be used with great care. Learning how to read them, then and now, is a lifelong task, requiring keen intuition as well as a comprehensive knowledge of Norse history and mythology.

Runes used for divination and meditation are typically made from a natural material such as wood or stone, each etched with a different symbol. Some runic symbols are named for animals, including elk and horse, and others for things found in nature, such as ice, hail, birch, and water. There's *tiwaz*, which is named after the warrior god Tyr, and *thurisaz*, which represents the race of giants. There are runes describing actions, such as riding a horse, and emotions, including joy. And some runes are named after human-made items: a torch, for example, and an ancestral hall.

As I delved deeper into books about the runes, I learned that each symbol has an entire set of symbolic associations rather than just a single meaning. *Fehu*, the first rune, signifies domestic cattle, which were an important source of wealth in the Viking Age. But if it comes up in your reading, it probably doesn't mean that a cow is going to come loping into your life but instead suggests money and abundance in some form, with an undertone of caution that this bounty must be used well or it can be problematic. Another rune, known as *eihwaz*, is connected to the yew, a tree often planted in graveyards. *Eihwaz* might indicate that a person is dealing with life-and-death issues or that they're in need of regeneration.

During that winter that began with my re-reading of the Norse myths, I spent much of my free time with the runes, memorizing their meanings and doing readings for myself and for friends. I came to enjoy the process of working with the runes, which reminded me of an intricate puzzle. Spreading them out on a white cloth before me, I thought of the Roman historian Tacitus watching the Norse warriors engaged in a similar activity. And as I cast my eye over the combinations of symbols, I had no trouble at all imagining I was looking into the well of knowledge that sits at the base of the world tree Yggdrasil, peering intently as I tried to discern the swirling patterns of *wyrd*.

WITH THE NORSE PAGANS

As a man wearing a set of antlers walked past me in the lobby of a suburban hotel in Minneapolis, I realized that Paganicon wasn't going to be like any conference I'd attended before.

I'd found its website while researching Norse pagans in the Midwest. Its description immediately piqued my interest: it was a gathering for "Pagans, Wiccans, Heathens, Druids and people of other folk, craft, indigenous or magickal traditions." Since it was held in Minneapolis, it sounded like it would be a good spot to connect with Kari Tauring. I wanted to learn more about her work and also how it fit into the larger pagan community in the Upper Midwest. Besides, attending a pagan convention sounded like a hoot, especially because I'd been a

Wiccan in my early twenties, a time when I cast off the Lutheranism of my childhood and set off on a lifetime of religious adventuring. It would be interesting to see what my old crowd was up to these days.

Sitting on a couch in the lobby, I browsed the Paganicon's schedule, which included three days of workshops, panels, and discussions, plus a costume ball, live music, and social gatherings. While many offerings related to this year's theme of Sacred Groves, other topics included Best Practices in Magickal Hygiene, Introduction to Familiar Spirits, and Egyptian Trance Dancing. The eclecticism of the offerings was mirrored in the free-spirited vibe of its participants, who in addition to the antlered man included several women sporting fairy wings, a gray-pony-tailed highlander clad in a kilt, and people wearing T-shirts with sayings such as "Hekate is my Homegirl" and "I'd Rather Be Skyclad." In my sensible pair of pants and nondescript sweater, I felt like I had the word *BORING* stamped on my forehead.

"It's too bad you missed last year when the conference theme was Norse spirituality," Kari told me when I met her for lunch later that day (I was relieved to see that she was dressed similarly to me, which proved that you didn't have to follow a dress code at the conference). "We're not as big a presence this year, but Paganicon always attracts a lot of people who draw inspiration from Norse pagan traditions."

At my request, Kari started our conversation with some background on her personal story, explaining that she'd grown up in a Minnesota family that strongly identified with its Norwegian heritage. She began studying Norse runes and mythology as an undergraduate, which led to years of research in the languages, poetry, and history of Scandinavia and the Norwegian immigrant experience in the United States. That, combined with her passion for music and dance, provided the basis for her reinterpretation of the ways of the staff-carrying women of her heritage and the development of the Völva Stav spiritual path. While she speaks and performs around the United States and abroad, she's most interested in giving people information that they can use for their own self-study and discovery. Her goal is to take ancient lore and pair it with more modern material, creating new interpretations of what it means to be Nordic.

According to Kari, the Minneapolis area has many people who affiliate with pre-Christian Scandinavian spirituality. Many belong to local worship and fellowship groups known as kindreds, while others are solitary practitioners. "Some people follow the Norse path exclusively, and some haven't given up their Lutheranism, me included," said Kari. "I'm not a practicing Lutheran, but I don't think I need to cut myself off from two thousand years of Christian *öorlog*, especially because I know there are things within Christianity that helped my immigrant ancestors to survive. You don't want to throw baby Jesus out with the bathwater, after all."

Given my own haphazard endeavors in genealogy, I was envious when Kari explained that she has a strong sense for her personal *öorlog* and knows her female lineage going back to the 1600s. "My deepest interest is my own family of origin, and I try to help my students do their own family-of-origin work," she said. "When people say they want to study with me, the first thing I have them do is write down their family tree. Who are their people? What are their languages? Where did they live? The foundation of Völva Stav is to get in touch with your own *öorlog* first."

The more Kari talked, the more I could see how her work shed new light on my own research on the interplay between genealogy and spirituality. I was especially interested in her explanation of the role of ancestors in traditional Scandinavian culture. "It's believed that our female ancestors are most connected to our everyday lives, and that male ancestors are more the overriding spirit of the family, but are less accessible on a day-to-day basis," she said. "Our female ancestors come to us when we're born, remain with us during our lifetimes, and guide us into our next life after our deaths. If you don't have a good relationship with them, it's said that they're sleeping. There are many Norse stories of people going into the underworld to wake up their ancestors so they can connect with them. That's one of the reasons that we need to maintain our connection to our ancestor spirits."

Kari's explanation of what she called the Web of Wyrd resonated as well. *Wyrd*, she said, is the energetic matrix that connects everything in the past and present, as well as future potential events. The web carries the record of everything that's happened, the emotional responses and resulting actions, of every living being. The lines originate in and eventually terminate in the Well of Urd at the base of the world tree Yggdrasil. (Urd is the Norn who oversees the past, you'll recall.) If that sounds hopelessly fanciful, she added, you can think of it as an ancient version of the string theory in quantum physics.

The English language has an echo of *wyrd*'s original meaning in our word *weird*. "In former times, a *wyrd* experience was one that seemed to have its origins in the numinous, in the world of the gods," Kari said. "It's an experience that causes the hair to rise on the back of your neck, or one that feels highly significant for some unknown reason. That gets to the deeper meaning of what *wyrd* once meant."

After I said goodbye to Kari, the concepts she'd talked about filled my thoughts. Her explanation of the Web of Wyrd applied to my own personal quest but also to genealogy in general. I thought of the family chart I'd seen many times on my computer screen, with its many branches and subbranches. It didn't take much imagination to picture that set of names as a web stretching further and further into the past, in the process connecting me to the *öorlog* of countless other people.

That image kept returning to me as I mingled with other people at the convention. I chatted with someone who gets messages from stones, and another who makes her living as a psychic. Of the Norse pagans I met, most had some Scandinavian in their ethnic mix, though not all. They gave a variety of reasons for affiliating with that tradition. Some were attracted by the mythology; others, by the camaraderie of the gatherings. One woman confessed that she probably wouldn't be a Norse pagan at all if it weren't for the weather in Minnesota. "Something about the cold and snow of winter makes it seem right to follow this path," she said. "It makes me wonder if there are any Norse pagans in Miami."

Later in the day I hung out with a group of Norse pagans from Wisconsin, who have their own acreage in a remote forest where they gather for ceremonies and potlucks. "It's a great way to raise kids," a man explained. "Everybody looks out for the little ones and all the families know one another."

The Norse pagans I met were friendly, hearty, and straightforward, even if some of them did sport fearsome-looking tattoos and prodigious beards. It was clear, too, that these people defined their kindred groups not by blood but by a common love for the Norse world. You might even say they were enthralled, to use that old Viking word that once meant enslaved.

As for myself, I was beginning to realize just how much more complex—and enthralling—genealogy could be if I stirred in some Viking Age metaphysics.

Stein and Tim Jorgensen dressed in Norse attire at the Midwest Viking Festival in Moorhead, Minnesota. (PHOTO BY LORI ERICKSON)

6

Living History

Several months later, an e-mail from Kari Tauring contained an invitation that generated nearly as much excitement in me as if I'd been offered an all-expenses-paid trip to Paris. "Are you interested in coming to a Viking reenactment in Moorhead, Minnesota, in June?" she wrote. "I could find you some clothes to wear. It might be useful for your book."

Oh, yes, I was interested. You're offering me the chance to dress up in Norse clothing and hang out with people who are as obsessed with the Viking Age as I am? What isn't there to like?

Bob, who often comes along with me on research trips, was quick to decline my suggestion that he join us. "I think I'm going to need to mow the lawn that weekend," he said.

"Our lawn takes ten minutes to mow," I said. "And aren't you intrigued by what it will be like? Just think of the conversations!"

"I don't have any trouble at all imagining what it will be like," Bob said. "I live with you."

The entire reenactor scene has long piqued my interest, even before Kari's invitation to the Scandinavian Hjemkomst and Midwest Viking Festival in Moorhead. Throughout the world—but especially in the United States and Europe—thousands of people spend their weekends traveling back in time, taking on the identities of Revolutionary War soldiers, World War II paratroopers, fur traders from the 1830s, medieval artisans, Renaissance dandies, and pioneer-era seamstresses. In London, the Tempus Fugitives practice Elizabethan swordsmanship, while in Caboolture, Australia, the annual Abbey Medieval Festival draws 1,000 participants and 30,000 spectators. As one participant told a newspaper reporter, "People love it because you've got weapons and you're allowed to beat the snot out of each other, plus there's also a strong cultural background."

For history buffs like myself, the chance to *live* history rather than just read about it can be irresistible. Part of what held me back from actually joining a group, however, was that I could never decide which era I wanted to join. Another problem was that in whatever period I chose, almost all of the good roles are taken by the men, who get to fight in mock battles while the women spin wool or make johnny cakes over a campfire.

Even though I'd likely be stuck in a sedate woman's role instead of swinging a broadsword, the Viking festival still intrigued me. I gave Kari my measurements via e-mail so that she could send them out to her friends who have Viking dresses. I hoped that whoever was my size was a woman of higher social standing so that I could wear at least a little bit of Norse bling.

It turns out that clothing is a big deal in the reenacting world because while there are a lot of details you don't want to get historically right—having missing teeth or intestinal parasites, for example—it's not as hard to put together a historically correct set of garments. On our three-hour car ride together from Minneapolis to Moorhead, Kari explained some of the nuances of Viking apparel. Almost all of it was made from wool or linen, she said, though the wealthy could purchase imported silks from Asia. Most people had very few clothes because it was so labor intensive to make them, and only the well-to-do could afford ornamentation such as decorative beads or jewelry made of silver or gold.

Reenactors get their kit, as it's often called, from a variety of sources. Some Vikings purchase their outfits, but the preferred method is to make your own, usually using machine-produced wool or linen but then doing the stitching by hand, following patterns based on archaeological findings. The clothing of that era wasn't fancy, but it was functional and comfortable, with men typically wearing tunics and pants while women had ankle-length dresses, sometimes with an overdress held up by brooches at the shoulders. (In other words, if you're into luxurious fabrics and elegant designs, forget the Vikings and go find a Renaissance group.)

"Women made clothing, but their textile skills were also essential to the boat trade," Kari told me. "It took seven hundred sheep to make the wool for a single longboat sail, for example, and almost all of that work would have been done by women. When a ship went down, men tried to save the sail first because it was the most valuable part of the vessel."

In our hotel room the next morning, I watched with interest as Kari put on her outfit. Over a shift of white linen she wore a red, wool overdress held up by two turtle-shaped, bronze brooches. Several strings of beads hung around her neck, and on her head she wore a blue hood edged with a decorative ribbon. In her hand she carried a staff, a symbol of her role as a *völva*, a spiritual leader in the Norse tradition.

"You look lovely," I said. "And formidable."

My own outfit was more utilitarian than hers: a dress of blue linen and a brown woolen shawl pinned together with a needle made of bone, plus a kerchief-style wrap for my hair. Looking in the mirror, I reminded myself of pictures of my elderly grandmother. With a sigh I tucked a lock of hair under the kerchief and tightened a rope belt around my waist.

"You're a good, solid, middle-of-the-road Viking woman," Kari said. "The blue linen indicates you're from a higher social class, and that brown blanket is special to me—it's handwoven and made of fine wool. And you look very authentic, too, except for the sandals, of course."

I looked down at my feet. No one had offered to lend me a pair of Viking shoes, so instead I had on a pair of athletic sandals, Kari having told me that it's better to wear something clearly anachronistic, such as eyeglasses, than create confusion by wearing something that people might mistake for being authentic, such as a pair of black leather shoes.

On our way out of the hotel we passed a group of people who were obviously headed to the same event we were—bearded men in tunics and women in dresses that looked a lot like mine, though some of them had elaborate beaded necklaces that showed either that they were stretching the authenticity boundary or that their menfolk had enjoyed a mighty successful season of raiding the summer before. People chatted animatedly to one another, and I remembered Kari saying that the Viking reenactors are a tight-knit community, often meeting at multiple events throughout the year. Seeing that the hotel clerk didn't raise an eyebrow at how we were dressed, I guessed that this Moorhead motel was used to hosting visiting Vikings.

The scene on the lawn outside the Hjemkomst Center was even more lively. Inside a circle formed by canvas tents, merchants and artisans in period attire sold their wares and demonstrated Viking Age crafts. I watched as a smith poured molten silver into a mold, creating a replica of a pendant found in a tenth-century Scandinavian grave. In the center of the encampment, several women were cutting vegetables for a pot of stew that simmered over an open fire, while nearby another woman worked at a large loom whose vertical threads were weighed down by stones. The scene didn't look entirely historically accurate, given the tourists milling around and the number of Vikings wearing eyeglasses, but it certainly looked Viking-*ish*, especially because a stave church loomed in the background, a replica of a twelfth-century church in Vik, Norway.

"You wander around all you like," Kari told me. "You know where to find me."

With gratitude I headed off, leaving Kari behind at a table where she'd set out some of the elements of her spiritual practice, including sprigs of plants, a piece of bone, a deer's antler, and a set of Norse runes etched on round pieces of wood. She'd been hired by the festival to talk to passersby about Norse spirituality and would also do a concert in the stave church the next afternoon. As for me, I intended to make the most of my time with my fellow Viking enthusiasts.

As Kari had said, they were indeed a friendly and welcoming lot, most of them hailing from the Midwest. While the majority were of Scandinavian descent, others had joined the community because they were fascinated by some aspect of Viking history. As people called out greetings to one another and exchanged news, I was struck by the family atmosphere. I learned that the wool merchant was expecting a baby and that the potter had spent the previous winter in Florida. (I bet many of the original Vikings would have done so, too, given the chance.) I bought a handmade piece of jewelry from a woman and her teenage daughters from Minot, North Dakota, and was introduced to Stein Jorgensen, an adorable five-year-old dressed in Viking attire whose father, Tim, coordinates the festival.

I was struck, too, by how people's outward appearance often didn't jibe with their day-to-day identities. A gray-haired woman working as a weaver was actually a physician, while her husband who was crafting a wooden barrel turned out to be a research scientist who specializes in superconductivity and cryogenics—not an occupation in high demand during the Viking Age. As we chatted, I learned more about Elspeth and Owen Christianson's background. They'd been involved in the Viking reenacting community since the 1970s and became so fascinated that they constructed a replica of a Viking Age house on their property in rural Wisconsin in 2011 using traditional materials and techniques. When they moved to the East Coast six years later, they donated the building to the University of Wisconsin–Green Bay, where it's now used as part of the school's history and humanities programs.

"So why did you decide to build a Viking house?" I asked them.

"If you could build a Viking house, wouldn't you?" Owen replied.

His question made me pause. "Well, I guess I would," I answered, unable to come up with a good reason not to.

Later in the morning, I met a man who said that his entry into Viking reenacting came through weaponry and battle demonstrations. He loved the camaraderie with the other men, he said, and the chance to test his physical limits. Though the fighting is carefully staged, considerable skill and strength are needed to wield heavy, dangerous weapons such as broad-swords and axes. (In fact, the next morning one of the men sustained a head injury during a practice session. When Kari inquired of a fellow reenactor later in the day how the injured man was doing, the man replied, "Which one?")

For many of the women, in contrast, the fiber arts seemed to be the major draw into the world of the Norse. I met several of them tending big tubs of hot water that were being used to color fabric with plant-based dyes. Nearby, I watched a woman demonstrate nalbinding, a form of one-needle weaving. The technique, which looked fiendishly complicated, creates a series of knots that don't unravel nearly as easily as a piece of knitting does. The woman told me that knitting with two needles didn't come into use until the thirteenth century, making me wonder about the first person to create one of those gorgeous sweaters that are ubiquitous in Scandinavia today.

Later in the afternoon, I attended a presentation on the making of linen by Heidi Sherman, who teaches history and humanities at the University of Wisconsin–Green Bay (where she makes good use of the Christianson's Viking house). She explained the laborious process by which the stringy fibers of the flax plant are cleaned and separated so that they can be woven. Afterward, she passed around a small square of linen she'd created from flax she'd grown herself. Looking at the unimpressive product that must have entailed hundreds of hours of work, I had a new appreciation for the miracle of machine-produced cloth.

As the day wore on, I amused myself by squinting a bit as I wandered the encampment, trying to focus just on the people in Viking attire and not the tourists. With a little effort, it didn't take much to imagine I was in a Scandinavian village a thousand years ago. I found myself thinking more deeply about what it would have been like to be a Norse woman, thoughts stimulated in part by my outfit, because while clothes make the man, they certainly make the woman as well. Walking across the lawn, the swing of my dress felt much different from the pants I typically wear, and the kerchief that had seemed so awkward at first was beginning to feel more natural. I regretted that no one had offered to lend me a set of Viking underwear, though I understood their hesitancy. (The archaeological evidence is unclear, but wealthier people probably wore loose-fitting linen undershirts). I imagined what it would be like to go through a harsh winter in the homespun clothes I was wearing.

My best moment came when I stopped by the cooking area, where a woman invited me to sample from the array of historically accurate foods they'd prepared, which included smoked trout, a flatbread made from freshly ground grains, and a hearty chicken stew. "Sample whatever you like," the cook said. "All the food here is for the Vikings." Her offer warmed my heart. For this festival, at least, I was truly a Viking, despite my modern sandals and underwear.

THE FOREIGN COUNTRY OF THE PAST

Even if you visit one just as a tourist, historical reenactments are one of the best ways to connect with our ancestors. Something about smelling the smoke of campfires, socializing with people dressed in the styles of a previous era, and seeing them use the tools of the past gives a visceral sense for what it was like for those who've gone before. The past is another country, but through events like these we can get hints of what it was like to live in it.

Before the twentieth century, historical reenactments in the United States and Europe were typically one-off events organized in recognition of a specific anniversary, often of a major battle. But in 1961, the hundredth anniversary of the start of the Civil War kick-started a more widespread movement. Over the next decades, Civil War reenacting attracted many thousands of enthusiasts and ignited interest in other historical eras as well. Today, there are hundreds of reenactor groups in the United States. Most people involved are hobbyists, but a lucky few are employed by historical sites to re-create the past for pay.

Most reenactors agree that they wouldn't like to *live* in the past; the wonders of vaccines, anesthesia, and modern sewer systems outweigh their commitment to fully experiencing historical eras down to every last detail. The contemporary world has its problems, to be sure, but a much higher percentage of humans today are wealthier, healthier, and better fed than has been true throughout recorded history. Even an ordinary middle-class American enjoys luxuries that the crowned heads of Europe had only recently.

While reenacting has often been associated with wars and battles, a younger generation seems more interested in the nonmartial arts. Our ancestors learned from their elders how to make pottery, hone flint into a sharp edge, and hunt wild game, skills that were essential for the majority of human history. A curious and hardy set of people in our own time want to reclaim that knowledge, whether or not their lives depend on it.

Heidi Sherman, the one who'd taught me about linen making, said that many of her college students are hungry for something concrete in their lives, activities that are tactile and grounded. "A growing number of young people are tired of having everything mediated through the digital world," she said. "They want to do things that are hands-on and real. They think it's fun to learn blacksmithing or weaving or mead brewing."

Historical reenacting always involves a certain amount of conjecture, and the further back in time you go, the more guesswork is required. That's why a passion for hands-on history has given birth to a discipline known as experimental archaeology, in which researchers test academic theories by trying them out in the real world. One of the early pioneers of this discipline was Thor Heyerdahl, who in 1947 sailed a raft he'd built based on ancient models from Peru to Polynesia (not from Norway to Iceland, as one might assume from his name). Others have constructed machines based on Leonardo da Vinci's designs and moved massive stones without modern equipment à la Stonehenge to try to figure out how prehistoric monuments were built. If you have a question about how something was done in the past, someone has almost certainly tried to find out the answer by actually doing it.

Browsing the Internet one day, I became fascinated by some of the many how-to videos that teach people so-called primitive skills (though seeing how complicated they are made me doubt the truth of that adjective). I watched a mud hut being built from scratch, learned how to tan a deer hide and make it into a pair of moccasins, saw a bison killed with an atlatl spear-thrower, and got slightly nauseated by a video of catching, roasting, and eating crickets. You don't have to go to a reenactment to learn about the past—simply click on YouTube instead.

While some reenactment events are private, allowing participants to dial up the authenticity meter to the max, the majority are public, in part because reenactors love to share their knowledge with the public. They've spent hundreds of hours doing research, after all, and wouldn't you like to sit down and hear how legs were amputated before anesthesia?

While the people I met in Moorhead were all interested in the Viking Age, I detected some differences in their approach to history. A number of them were affiliated with the Minnesota Renaissance Festival and the Society for Creative Anachronism, groups that don't have the same degree of commitment to historical accuracy as most Viking reenactors. At the same time, even hard-core history buffs recognize that everyone has to start somewhere. Those who enter the reenacting world with a casual interest often become more concerned with accuracy later on.

Whatever the period being portrayed, reenacting can be expensive. A well-equipped Civil War soldier, for example, needs a tent, uniform, canteens, cooking utensils, pistol, and rifle (the rifle alone can cost more than $1,000). The most conscientious of history buffs try to find things that not only *look* accurate but were also *made* accurately. Hearing about some of the ways Civil War reenactors try to be authentic, including starving themselves to appear appropriately gaunt, made me feel guilty about my own Viking experience, appreciative as I was of the warm shower and comfortable bed in the hotel room that Kari and I shared, which I'm happy to say had nary a bedbug or flea, despite the historical inaccuracy.

Another potentially sticky area is the relationship between history enthusiasts and professional historians, which has similarities to the relationship between people interested in genealogy and those for whom history is an academic discipline. Some of their goals and methods may overlap, but their paths often diverge. A common criticism by historians is that reenactors focus so much on getting the details of history correct— the type of buttons on uniforms, for example, or the thread count in clothing—that they ignore the larger cultural and social realities of the period.

While I can understand that concern, my time among the Vikings both reinforced my fascination with the Norse world and gave me an experiential sense for some of its day-to-day realities. It also helped explain why the long list of names and dates on Ancestry.com didn't do much for me: what interests me about my ancestors are the stories of their individual lives and the cultural and political forces that shaped them. While historical research is important, my imagination remains my primary tool for accessing the past.

NORSE FOR THE LOVE OF IT

Some of my best conversations with my fellow Vikings took place at dinner on the first evening of the festival. Released from the need to interact with tourists, they had more time to chat as they tucked into a catered meal of Mediterranean specialties served in an outdoor beer garden next to the stave church (no one seemed bothered by the incongruity of eating hummus, falafel, and kebabs while dressed as Vikings).

I took a seat across the table from Elspeth and Owen Christianson, the couple who'd constructed a Viking longhouse on their property, while next to me sat the silversmith whom I'd met earlier in the day at his forge. As we dined, I asked them what they thought real Vikings would think of a reenactment like the one we were attending. They laughed. "They'd think we were crazy," the smith said. "They'd view this as a total waste of time." The four of us amused ourselves by speculating on what they would be interested in instead, finally concluding that the ordinary Vikings would likely join the military to improve their social standing and economic opportunities, while the chieftains, the ones who led and financed the raids, would probably head to New York to become wolves on Wall Street.

As the beer flowed, the conversations got more animated, and I was struck again by the warm atmosphere of the gathering. The Norse were big on clan, and it felt a bit like a clan here as people moved from one table to another to visit and get caught up on one another's lives. Even if some of them were camped in tents and wimps like me were staying in hotels, we were united by our shared sense of wanting something more than just our technology-obsessed world. Learning how to make linen from flax or fight with a broadsword doesn't make much practical sense (unless, of course, modern society collapses, and then all of us are going to wish we had reenactor friends who will take us in). But enthusiasts like these Vikings pursue their studies of history and craft for the sheer enjoyment of it. It wasn't just their clothing that was authentic— *they* seemed more authentic, too.

The next day, I ventured farther afield at the festival, which celebrates all things Danish-Norwegian-Swedish-Finnish-Icelandic, a reflection of the region's many residents who trace their heritage to Scandinavia. The Hjemkomst Center (the name comes from a Norwegian word meaning *homecoming*) has been hosting the event since 2008. In addition to the stave church on its grounds, the center also has a replica of a Viking ship built by Robert Asp, a Moorhead Junior High School guidance counselor who first had the idea in 1971. In 1982, a dozen hardy souls sailed it to Norway, retracing the journey of the region's ancestors.

In the festival's dining area, large signs proclaimed the ethnicity of the foods for sale, including Norwegian *lefse*, *rømmegrøt*, and *lutefisk*; Finnish rhubarb soup; Swedish almond cake; and Icelandic smoked salmon on brown bread. The Danes, meanwhile, were hawking addictive little pancake balls known as *abelskivers*.

After sampling some of the delicacies, I wandered amid the displays set up around the Viking longboat and outside the building. I visited with a man who was demonstrating a Hardanger fiddle, an ornately decorated instrument that has eight strings rather than the standard four, and I met a couple who had two Norwegian elk hounds at their side, one named Freya and the other Odin. I debated whether I should buy a canvas bag bearing the image of a kitten wearing a horned Viking helmet or a T-shirt with the saying "It takes a Viking to raze a village." The only non-Scandinavian offering at the festival was a booth with bathroom remodeling products staffed by a woman wearing an outfit similar to Xena Warrior Princess (her employer was clearly more interested in commerce than history).

Growing a little weary, I was happy to find a seat inside the stave church, which hosted a full slate of programs throughout the festival. I listened as Adrian Spendlow, a professional storyteller whose accent reveals his British heritage, shared tales from Norse mythology that brought Odin and Loki vividly to life. In talking with him afterward, I learned that he works at a Norwegian living history site known as Viking Village for part of the year, where he's the *skald*, or court poet, to its chieftain.

"I've never had my DNA done, but coming from the city of York in England, I'd be surprised if I didn't have any Viking DNA," he told me, which led to a conversation about my own recent experiences in York. When I told him about being related to Leif Eriksson, he seemed suitably impressed and said he'd be sure to tell his chieftain about meeting me.

I took my seat again and looked around the church, savoring its beauty. Built of wood, it blends medieval church architecture with traditional Norse elements such as ornate decorative carvings inside and dragon heads on its steeply pitched roof. I found it appropriate that in trying to connect with their heritage, the people of this area showcase two iconic symbols: a ship that represents the fierce world of the Vikings and a church that evokes the much better-behaved culture that later came to dominate Scandinavia. If Norwegian Americans have a communal astrological sign, it would be Gemini, twins whose dual nature can adapt to almost any circumstance.

Kari Tauring was next on the festival schedule. I closed my eyes for much of her performance, both tired and wanting to sink into the sound of her ethereal voice. She chanted and sang songs from a variety of Norse traditions, some of which dated back hundreds of years. I couldn't understand the languages she was singing, but something in them was mesmerizing, hinting of cold and snow and mountains. When she finished, I opened my eyes and was slightly surprised to find myself sitting in Minnesota.

NEEDED: HISTORY FANS

While the Viking reenactor scene seems to be doing well (there are even groups in South America), other time periods are finding it hard to recruit new members—a fact I learned a month later when I visited the Fort Laramie National Historic Site in Wyoming, one of the most important locations in the history of European westward expansion and Native American resistance in the United States. Founded by fur traders in the 1830s, the fort later protected immigrants on the Oregon, California, and Mormon Trails and was the site of the signing of several important treaties with indigenous tribes.

Reenactors used to be plentiful at Fort Laramie, according to a park ranger I spoke to. But in recent years their numbers have dwindled as older members fade from the scene and are not replaced by a new generation. "Young people don't have the same interest in history that they used to," he said. "They're not taught much of it in school, and their parents don't have as much time to take them to historic sites on vacation. Two decades ago, we used to get more than 100,000 visitors a year, and now it's less than 50,000. We once had lots of people who came here and said they've wanted to visit Fort Laramie their entire lives. Now that happens very rarely."

When Bob and I retreated from the hot sun to refresh ourselves with a couple of old-fashioned sodas at the fort's trading post, we met another employee who agreed that interest in history is fading somewhat in American culture—though it certainly wasn't the case with him. With his full beard, old-fashioned shirt and vest, and cowboy hat, the man looked every inch a nineteenth-century bartender, despite his upbringing on the outskirts of Boston. For him, a childhood fascination with the frontier era eventually led to a job working at this historic site in Wyoming. "I'm an Italian city boy, but I've always been interested in the Old West," he said. "When people asked me what I wanted to be when I grew up, I'd say I wanted to own a big herd of cattle."

As I sipped my drink, the two of us bonded over our shared interest in genealogy. His wife is descended from Scottish royalty, he said, launching into a detailed description of her family tree that I must admit made my mind wander a bit. But I had to smile at the incongruity of it all, standing there at a bar straight out of *Deadwood* talking to an Italian dressed up like a cowboy who was telling me about his links to the Scottish royal family. The Web of Wyrd does indeed show up in unexpected places, and I felt a connection to this man, who'd also fallen in love with a historical era.

Walking across the parade ground of the fort, I thought back to my experience among the reenactors at the Viking festival. Their era was enjoying a renaissance of interest, helped in large part by media blockbusters including *Frozen* and *Game of Thrones*. Interest in the Old West, in contrast, is declining, proving that fashion is part of the reenacting world as much as the real world. Today Viking warriors are in; perhaps in a few years cowboys will come riding back. Or maybe they won't, because the make-believe worlds of shoot-'em-up video games and superhero movies seem to have much greater allure in popular culture.

I remembered something that the ranger had said. "I often think of that line that says those who don't remember history are doomed to repeat it," he said. "The Old West had its problematic aspects—its treatment of the native peoples, especially. But it also is a vital part of American history, full of dramatic and fascinating events. It would be a shame if fewer and fewer people learn that story."

I thought of the Vikings I'd met at the festival, that industrious crew who love learning the skills from a millennia ago, and felt a sense of gratitude that in their corner of the reenacting world, at least, history is being kept alive.

By mid-afternoon of the second day of the Viking festival, I had to admit that some of my enthusiasm was waning. My kerchief kept slipping out of place, and it startled me every time I went to the bathroom and realized how old I looked dressed as a Viking woman. I'd met most of the reenactors and sampled all the ethnic treats I was interested in, nearly every one of them involving some variation of butter, cream, and white flour. And when I stepped back outside, I discovered to my dismay that the weather had taken a turn for the worse. A cold wind was blowing, and it was starting to rain, a cold drizzle that looked like it was going to last the rest of the day.

I wandered back into the village, where the tourists had mostly disappeared and some of the vendors were putting away their wares. As the minutes passed, the lawn got muddier, and the rain, colder. I was getting colder, too, despite pulling the wool shawl tighter around my shoulders. My sandals were soaked, and my toes were chilly. I looked at my watch, surreptitiously. When I saw that there were two more hours to go before the festival ended, I heaved a big sigh.

And then I had a thought: you know, I wasn't *really* a Viking woman. While being chilled, damp, and miserable was probably the single most authentic thing about the Viking festival, I was also a resident of the twenty-first century. Feeling a little ashamed of myself, I asked Kari for the car keys and scrounged in the back of the vehicle for my regular clothes. Changing into them inside the museum's bathroom, I savored the feel of warm socks and dry shoes. With pleasure I took off the irritating kerchief and tried my best to rescue my hairstyle. I put on some lipstick, enjoying the sight of red color on my lips again, and then put on a raincoat and headed out into the rain, this time much better equipped against the weather.

Walking back through the village, I admired all the Vikings who were continuing to cook, weave, card wool, and talk to the dwindling number of tourists. They were showing much more fortitude than I was. But I, in contrast to them, was dry and warm. I let myself into the car, sat in the front seat, and opened up my laptop. I had time to get some work done before Kari would be ready to leave at 5:00 p.m. Never had I been so happy to catch up on e-mails.

The Kensington Rune Stone, on display in Alexandria, Minnesota, has stirred controversy ever since it was discovered in a farmer's field in 1898. (PHOTO BY BOB SESSIONS)

7

The Perils of Mythmaking

-:✳:-

On a late summer's day in 1898, a Swedish immigrant named Olof Ohman was uprooting a poplar tree from a field in his farm in central Minnesota when he found something that would become an object of fascination for his home state—and at times the rest of the nation—for decades. Entangled in the tree roots was a three-foot-tall slab of gray rock that had Norse runes chiseled on its surface. Similarly carved stones had been found in Scandinavia, but never in North America. When translated, the inscription told of an expedition of Norsemen (eight Swedes and twenty-two Norwegians) who traveled from "Vinland to the west" in 1362. One day some of the men went fishing. When they returned to camp, they found ten of their comrades "red of blood and dead." The rune stone rewrote established history by proving that Scandinavian explorers had penetrated much farther into the interior of the continent than previously realized.

Or maybe not. Because almost certainly the rune stone is a hoax.

The Kensington Rune Stone raises the issue of the relationship between genealogy and mythology. In many families, some of the most-treasured stories shade the truth. Instead of serving on a battleship in the Pacific during World War II, your grandfather might have spent his time in the Navy working in a stateside warehouse. Maybe your mother's second cousin didn't dance with the Rockettes, but instead kicked and shimmied in burlesque shows. That story about your grandfather being a close friend of Thomas Edison? Quite likely untrue, though they might have lived in the same town at one point. Many of us have the impulse to embellish the past, especially when there's no one around to correct us (full disclosure: that story about my cousin dying of gangrene in his butt after sitting on a dirty fork probably isn't true either).

These shadings of the truth muddy the historical record, whether they're told by individuals, professional genealogists, or researchers with an agenda. But the stories we tell, and our willingness to suspend our skepticism when we hear a tale we want to believe, reveal a lot about who we are and what's important to us. And during the late nineteenth and early twentieth centuries, many Minnesotans wanted to believe that the Vikings had been in the state several centuries before the first Scandinavian pioneers arrived.

The cult of Leif Eriksson (as historian Odd Lovoll charmingly refers to the fascination some people have with my ancestor) had many enthusiastic members in Minnesota during those years. A large percentage of the state's citizens were of Norwegian and Swedish stock, and they loved reading stories about how their hardy forefather landed in North America long before Christopher Columbus.

While most historians believed that Eriksson's Vinland settlement had been in Canada, some reputable scholars surmised that the Vikings also journeyed farther south, traveling from the coast of Newfoundland into modern-day New England. The Kensington Rune Stone gave credence to the idea that the Scandinavians had gone even farther west in their wanderings. These explorers were soon dubbed Vikings, even though the Viking Age ended several centuries before the rock was supposedly carved. The rune stone was welcomed in part because it gave reassuring proof that the immigrant Scandinavians weren't strangers in a strange land after all: their ancestors had been in Minnesota a long time ago.

The story of the Kensington Rune Stone is one of the most peculiar chapters in Midwestern history. No one ever publicly confessed to creating the hoax. Nobody made much money off of it. And other than a few rogue scholars and eccentrics, no expert has ever declared it authentic. But the story has taken on a life of its own, influencing several generations and leading many to conclude to this day that even if the rune stone is a fake, it's probably true that the Vikings roamed in Minnesota at some point. Such is the power of myth—and if you doubt this, go to the Minnesota Vikings football stadium in Minneapolis to see the Norse ship at its entrance.

One of the many strange parts of the saga of the Kensington Rune Stone is how it became intertwined with efforts to promote Christianity, in particular, Catholicism. The original Vikings, after all, were worshipers of Odin, Thor, and the rest of the Norse pantheon. But the runes on the stone include three Latin letters: *AVM*, which come just after the part about the men being found "red of blood and dead." Some thought the letters referred to *Ave Virgo Maria*, which would make this Hail Mary not a forward pass at the end of a Vikings game but the first written Christian prayer in North American history.

Speculating further, some connected the rune-stone expedition with a story from the court of King Magnus of Sweden, a Catholic who was so worried about the Norse Greenlanders lapsing into worship of pagan gods that in 1354 he proposed an expedition to try to reconvert them. There's no evidence that his plan was ever carried out, but the story gelled nicely with the tale of the Vikings in Minnesota. The men had wandered far from their original destination of Greenland, but they were still looking for people to convert to Christianity, bless their hearts.

The supposed history of the rune stone eventually got so convoluted that one must simply sit back and admire the filigree. This is especially true for someone like me, who grew up in a world in which there were Norwegian Lutherans and Swedish Lutherans and Danish Lutherans, groups divided by country of origin and language and doctrinal variations, but all united in a shared distrust of Catholicism. I wish I could have been a fly on the wall when the Minnesota Lutherans first heard that the Rune Stone Vikings were being proclaimed as the first Catholic martyrs in North America.

After church officials declared the rune stone a Catholic artifact, a parochial school in Alexandria, Minnesota, set up a shrine of the Virgin Mary standing with her hands outstretched next to a replica of the rune stone. In 1964, a new Catholic church named Our Lady of the Runestone was dedicated in the town of Kensington near where the stone was found. Diocesan media carried stories about the Catholic background of the famed historical relic, and church leaders trumpeted the news widely in hopes it might convince some wavering Lutherans to convert. Instead, considerable pearl clutching ensued. Many Lutherans didn't take kindly to the idea that their stouthearted ancestors had not only prayed to the Virgin Mary in their time of distress, but also made sure everyone remembered their heresy by carving it in stone. It's unlikely that many conversions to Catholicism happened because of the Kensington Rune Stone.

While most scholars continued to believe that the rune stone was a nineteenth-century hoax (a verdict made primarily on the basis of a linguistic analysis of the runes), it still attracted considerable national attention. In 1948–49 the stone was displayed at the Smithsonian Institution, and in 1964–65 it was part of the Minnesota exhibition at the New York World's Fair. National media featured articles on it, from *Harper's Weekly* and the *Saturday Evening Post* to *National Geographic*. In a poll taken in 1963, 60 percent of Minnesotans believed that Vikings were the first European visitors to their state.

Much of the credit for the rune stone's fame goes to amateur historian Hjalmar Holand, a Norwegian immigrant who devoted his life to proving its authenticity and promoting its fame. While his assertions skirted the edge of probability, other enthusiasts made even grander claims. One researcher wrote that it contained "secret calendrical [sic] data pertaining to the perpetual calendar of the Catholic Church." Another deciphered coded messages in its inscription, discovering not only the names of all the members of the expedition but also a reference to a gopher, the Minnesota state mascot.

By this point, it should come as no surprise that some people believe the Rune Stone Vikings were members of the Knights Templar and that they were carrying the Holy Grail on their trip through Minnesota.

The high point of the rune-stone story came in 1962. To celebrate the six-hundredth anniversary of the artifact's supposed creation, the town of Alexandria (which is located fifteen miles northeast of where the stone was found) staged a spectacular outdoor pageant with a cast of more than fifty. The show included scenes of King Magnus launching a holy crusade, Vikings arriving on a dragon-headed ship, the untimely deaths of their comrades, and Norse goddesses galloping on real horses across the stage to pick up the fallen warriors while Richard Wagner's "Ride of the Valkyries" played over the loudspeakers. Occasionally, an actor portraying Hjalmar Holand came onto the stage to defend the rune stone's authenticity and decry the pointy-headed academics who pooh-poohed it. And at the end, a spotlight shone on a lone Viking warrior carving on a stone. Behind him stood the goddess Columbia holding an American flag and the Norse goddess Brunhilde brandishing a spear and sword, while to the sides were women carrying the flags of Sweden and Norway.

It was all so thrilling that it didn't make much difference whether any of it was true.

A STORIED STONE

When I told a friend in Minneapolis that I was going to visit the town of Alexandria, she immediately guessed why. "Oh, please tell me you're not going to see the Kensington Rune

Stone!" she exclaimed. "That thing is a fake. Everybody goes to see it, but it's still an embarrassment to the state."

But in the world of tourism, towns go with the historical gifts they've been given, including slightly suspect ones dug up in a farmer's field. Today Alexandria continues to embrace its most famous artifact with enthusiasm. In addition to businesses that include Nordic Trails Golf Course, Viking Pawn, Runestone Heating and Air Conditioning, and Viking Bank, it's the proud home of Big Ole, a 28-foot, four-ton, fiberglass statue that stands near the entrance to the Kensington Runestone Museum. The red-bearded giant was constructed to draw attention to the rune stone exhibit at the New York World's Fair. In one hand he holds a spear; in the other he bears a shield with the words "Alexandria: Birthplace of America." A raised platform a short distance away provides a place to take pictures, perfectly positioned to capture Big Ole in all his glory.

I entered the museum just behind a busload of chattering elementary school kids, who were being herded by several blond-haired women I assumed were teachers and chaperoning mothers. To kill time while they got their tickets, I browsed the gift shop, which sold Scandinavian-themed knickknacks and books relating to the rune stone and Nordic history, from *The Kensington Rune Stone: Compelling New Evidence* to *The Runestone: "Them Boys Was Here Alright!"* The latter subtitle, I learned from book's back cover, was a quote from Edward Ohman, the son of the farmer who discovered the rune stone. I admired his emphatic certainty.

Stepping inside the museum a few minutes later, I got the chance to see the famous stone in person. For an artifact that's stirred up such controversy and passion through the years, it looked surprisingly unassuming. Protected in a case, it's a bit battered around the edges—not surprising considering that for several years it served as a stepping-stone into a granary on the Ohman farm. Chiseled runes slanted across its surface, a jumble of Norse-looking script that looked pretty convincing, at least to my untrained eye.

As I stood gazing at it, trying to fully savor the moment, I noticed a white-haired woman with an intense gaze buttonholing a nearby guide. "I'm writing a book about the rune stone," she explained, then launched into a long description of how she was going to devote her retirement to the project. Remembering the shelves full of books in the gift shop, I wondered if I should take a number ("Now serving author number 87," says the announcement over the museum's loudspeaker).

"Is it true?" the woman asked. "The rune stone, I mean?"

The guide's answer was diplomatic. "The question of whether the rune stone is authentic will never be answered to everyone's satisfaction," she said. "But we do know that the man who discovered it, Olof Ohman, certainly didn't benefit from it. In fact, he and his family were ridiculed, because many people thought Olof had forged the inscription. One of his sons left the area because he couldn't handle the controversy, and another of his children, a daughter, committed suicide."

Her words made me look at the rune stone with new eyes. As innocuous as it seemed, the artifact had set in motion a cascade of far-reaching effects—again, proof of the power of a story. I decided against revealing my own writing project, a little hesitant to join the literary bandwagon, and instead eavesdropped on their conversation, which soon turned to a display of other possible Norse artifacts that had been found in the region. The most convincing, the guide said, was a fire steel (a tool used for starting fires) believed to date from the Middle Ages. It was found on the bank of the Red River near Climax, Minnesota, in 1871. I peered at the palm-sized, C-shaped piece of iron with interest, but it wasn't nearly as impressive as the slab of etched stone.

After viewing a short film on the rune stone's discovery (which lightly skipped over the controversy relating to its authenticity), I toured the museum's other exhibits, which included displays on the Ojibwe and Dakota heritage of the region—honoring the people who were here, of course, long before any white settlers and who suffered greatly after their arrival. Outside, a wooden, stockade-style fence enclosed a grassy area that held a pioneer-era church, schoolhouse, and general store as well as a building with another display relating to the rune stone: a forty-foot-long recreation of a Viking ship.

Built by the American Museum of Natural History in consultation with the Viking Ship Museum of Roskilde, Denmark, the vessel is a three-quarter-size replica of an eleventh-century, ocean-going, merchant ship from Norway. Walking slowly around it, I admired its sleek lines, expertly crafted wooden planks, and large sail, only partly unfurled because even the large building couldn't contain its full height. I remembered seeing similar replicas at L'Anse aux Meadows and at the Viking Festival in Moorhead. The boat looked like it was eager to escape the bonds of earth, straining to leap into the nearest waterway. A small sign said its name was *Snorri*, after the first European child born in North America. I was pleased to see that Gudrid the Far Traveler's son was being honored here in Minnesota, far from the coast of Canada where he was born.

The Kensington Rune Stone is almost certainly a fake. And in a sense, the boat is too. But both of them contain a kind of truth as well, reinforcing the fact that the ties between Minnesota and Scandinavia are old, strong, and more than a little quirky.

I had one more stop to make before leaving the area: the farm where the rune stone was found. As I drove through a rolling landscape of farms, small lakes, and woodlands, I had a sense of traveling back in time, back to that August day in 1898 when Olof Ohman set out to remove a tree from one of his fields and changed his life forever.

The Kensington Rune Stone Park preserves the Ohman farmstead as a time capsule of rural life from more than a century ago, with a red barn and white clapboard house set amid tall trees. A nearby visitor center, newly constructed, looks a little out of place in the bucolic setting, but its displays give an informative overview of why this out-of-the-way spot became famous. One window frames a view of the spot where the stone was found, now a nondescript hillside covered with grass.

I was intrigued by the visitor center's description of Olof Ohman's life. In Sweden, his father belonged to a class of people prohibited by law from owning land. Wanting to improve his lot in life, Olof sailed to America when he was twenty-four, eventually becoming a farmer in central Minnesota, a region that looked similar to the part of Sweden where he'd spent his early years. His story mirrored that of thousands of immigrants, then and now. In his homeland, his prospects were severely limited by poverty, tradition, and rigid political and social structures. In America, he could be anybody—including someone who set in motion a controversy that would attract international attention.

Looking out the window at the place where the rune stone was found, I realized that I didn't much care who'd created it—whether it was carved by fourteenth-century Scandinavian warriors or a nineteenth-century forger. What was more interesting to me, by far, was the way the stone had taken on a life of its own, launching quixotic theories, dividing public opinion, and pitting the true believers against the academics. I remembered hearing at the museum that a Swedish film crew had recently visited Alexandria as part of a search for medieval Scandinavian artifacts in Minnesota. The saga of the rune stone lives on because it's just too good a story to let die.

THE SINGING VIKINGS

It's time to talk about helmets with horns. You know the kind— the ones worn by the Vikings in the *Hagar the Horrible* comic strip and by frat boys at keg parties. If you want to get Norse scholars agitated, just ask them about this type of headgear, which has become the de rigueur image for Vikings despite an utter lack of historical confirmation. Instead, warriors either went bareheaded into battle or else wore simple leather or iron head coverings. A horned helmet, after all, would be awkward and dangerous to wear in combat, easily tipped off and as likely to put out the eye of a comrade as an enemy.

The bihorned headgear entered the popular imagination because of opera, not archaeology. In 1876, costume designer Carl Emil Doepler put horned helmets on some of the cast of *Der Ring des Nibelungen*, an opera cycle composed by Richard Wagner. Doepler was probably inspired by nineteenth-century archaeological discoveries of similar headgear, though later research indicated that they'd been created before the Viking Age, and that even then they'd probably been used only for ceremonial or ritual purposes.

The anachronistic helmets, however, are the least of the problems associated with the Wagner operas. That's because Richard Wagner was a vocal anti-Semite as well as a brilliant musician—and after his death, his music and writings attracted the admiration of Adolf Hitler. To this day, Wagner's music carries an asterisk because of its association with the Nazis.

In his glory days, however, Richard Wagner was one of the most celebrated composers in Europe, creating lush, soaring operas that packed houses and thrilled audiences. His most famous work is an interconnected set of operas known as the *Ring Cycle*, a four-part, eighteen-hour production that blends Norse, Icelandic, and German mythology. The story is epic, with gods and goddesses, a cursed ring, magic sword, dragon, dwarves, and giants. Lauded for its visionary blend of music and drama, Wagner's work deeply influenced the course of Western music.

Wagner continues to have an influence, despite his posthumous association with the Nazis. The "Ride of the Valkyries," for example, is one of the best-known pieces of music in the world, popping up everywhere from *Apocalypse Now* to Bugs Bunny cartoons (as well as the dramatic scene in the Kensington Rune Stone pageant when the Norse goddesses gallop off with the bodies of the Catholic Viking martyrs). His brilliant use of music to amplify emotion is emulated in countless forms of media. If you've ever sat riveted in a movie as dramatic music thunders through the theater, you're benefiting from the legacy of Richard Wagner.

During the eighteenth and nineteenth centuries, Wagner was just one among many people inspired by Norse culture and history. The so-called Viking Revival led authors, artists, musicians, and scholars throughout Europe to reinterpret the old traditions for a new age. During an era when nationalism was in the air and indigenous folk traditions were being celebrated, it's not surprising that the Vikings would be dusted off and brought down from the attic. This was particularly true in Scandinavia, where the Danes and Swedes were still smarting after humiliating military defeats by the Russians and British. They latched onto their Viking ancestors partly as a way to assert their national pride.

In Britain, meanwhile, many saw the Vikings as proto-Victorians: stern, courageous, and hardworking, just the sort of ancestors you'd want to have in your gene pool. It was even said that the British-Hanoverian royal line was descended from the Viking chief Ragnar Hairy-Breeches, which is better, I guess, than being descended from Thorfinn Skullsplitter, another chief. At Oxford, J. R. R. Tolkien was immersing himself in the study of Old Norse and the Icelandic sagas, efforts that, as I've said, would inspire a fantasy series that would far eclipse his scholarly reputation (the similarities between his epic and that of Wagner is that they used similar source materials). Archaeologists, meanwhile, were busy digging up new artifacts that shed light on the actual Vikings, not just their myths and stories. It was, in short, a good time to be fascinated by the Vikings.

It was during this era that "Viking Age" was first used to describe the period between 793 and 1066. When the warriors were actually roaming around, contemporaries outside of Scandinavia generally referred to them as the Northmen or heathen. While the exact words of the prayer "From the fury of the Northmen, O Lord, deliver us" are probably apocryphal, similar prayers were undoubtedly said by worried coastal-dwelling people throughout Europe.

This fascination with the Vikings took a much darker turn when the Nazi party rose to power in the 1930s. Among

Hitler's many obsessions was his idea of an Aryan race, a myth-
ical group of which the German and Nordic peoples were said
to be the purest examples. Fair-haired, blue-eyed men and
women—the sort of people you'd find walking around the
streets of Oslo—were said to be the true ancestors of the Third
Reich and the ideal physical type. It was a bitter fabrication
indeed for the Norwegians, who suffered greatly during the
Nazi occupation of their country from 1940–45.

To this day, some neo-Nazi and other white supremacist
groups claim a connection to Viking heritage and symbolism,
much to the horror of contemporary Scandinavians and those
of us who trace our roots to the northern lands. Historians are
also indignant, pointing out the ridiculousness of lauding the
Vikings as a "pure race." Almost everywhere they traveled, they
showed little concern for purity of dogma or tribe and often
enthusiastically adapted the customs of the local culture. Anyone who holds the Vikings up as a model of white supremacy
doesn't know their actual history.

The issue gained international attention in 2018 when a
controversy erupted over the sweaters worn by the Norwegian
alpine ski team at the Winter Olympics in Pyeongchang, South
Korea. The knitted design included the *tyr* rune, an arrow
pointing upward that's associated with the warrior god Tyr.
By extension, it's become a symbol of strength and bravery—a
quite appropriate emblem for the team, officials thought. A
media furor ensued, however, when it was pointed out that the
tyr rune is also a favorite symbol of some extremist groups. The
team was given another set of sweaters to wear, but many in
Norway lamented the fact that once again part of their heritage
was being appropriated and tainted by evildoers.

Those who organize reenactments also have to be on the
lookout for those attracted to the dark side of the Norse myth,
a fact that I learned at the Viking festival in Moorhead, where
they are hypervigilant about policing their ranks for anyone
who expresses sympathy for white supremacist causes. "It's
infuriating," one person told me. "These people twist Viking
history and use it to promote an ideology that the rest of us

find abhorrent. We don't want to be associated in any way with those people."

THE POWER OF MYTH

The controversy makes me reconsider some of my own myth-making about my heritage. By now it should be clear that I'm not exactly wedded to historical accuracy in genealogy—in fact, I'm a huge fan of creating the stories that help us form our identities, even if there's some artistic license involved. But I also realize there are problems with this approach (exhibit A: those white supremacists who claim Vikings as role models).

The problem with myths is that they're both vital to a culture and susceptible to misuse. Humans have been making myths since we first discovered language, stories that help make sense out of the swirling chaos of our lives. They help people find their place in the world and give them ideals to aspire to. Think of how stories about an obscure Welsh chieftain gave birth to the heroic King Arthur myth, or how Homer spun the history of the Trojan War into *The Iliad*. Myths like these can serve vital roles in uniting and inspiring groups of people. They work on a personal level, too, because all of us in recalling our personal histories gain from seeing ourselves as the hero, rather than the victim, of our lives. The hero's journey takes many forms, in other words, both for individuals and for cultures.

Karen Armstrong, a scholar of comparative religion, says that our modern alienation from myth is unprecedented. For most of human history, myths helped people make sense of their lives and revealed regions of the human mind that would otherwise have remained inaccessible. The stories of gods and goddesses descending into the underworld or fighting monsters brought to light the mysterious workings of the psyche, she says, and showed people how to cope with their own crises. That's why when Sigmund Freud and Carl Jung began to chart the modern quest for the soul, they turned to classical mythology to explain their insights, reinvigorating the old stories once again.

"A myth, therefore, is true because it is effective, not because it gives us factual information," writes Armstrong in *A Short History of Myth*. She continues:

> If, however, it does not give us new insights into the deeper meaning of life, it has failed. If it *works*, that is, if it forces us to change our minds and hearts, gives us new hope, and compels us to live more fully, it is a valid myth. Mythology will only transform us if we follow its directives. A myth is essentially a guide; it tells us what we must do in order to live more richly. If we do not apply it to our own situation and make the myth a reality in our own lives, it will remain as incomprehensible and remote as the rules of a board game, which often seem confusing and boring until we start to play.

Armstrong's words helped me make sense of my conundrum. The neo-Nazi myth is profoundly negative in its consequences, while the Kensington Rune Stone is mostly harmless. And if my own musings on Leif Eriksson and Gudrid the Far Traveler help me understand myself better and live a richer life, then the mythmaking I'm doing is probably just fine.

I also loved Armstrong's comparison to a board game, which made me think of one of my favorite Norse runes: *pertho*. It's one of the most ambiguous of the runes, and its full meaning is the subject of some debate. At one level it's associated with gaming and, by extension, with happiness, laughter, and fellowship. But at a deeper level, *pertho* is related to the idea of sacred play, the concept that in a game, we can see a reflection of the divine. The Norse gods themselves were playful, and in playing games we emulate them and can gain insights into divine consciousness.

The Vikings—who fought hard, worked hard, and played hard—loved games of all sorts, from gambling and board games to athletic events and drinking games. It likely seemed obvious to them that their gods would communicate with them through games. In throwing inscribed pieces on a cloth, they opened a window into another world. The runes thus became sacred play, a way of discerning the individual threads in the Web of Wyrd. In *Nordic Runes: Understanding, Casting, and Interpreting the Ancient Viking Oracle*, Paul Rhys Mountfort writes how contemporary rune casting (the kind Kari Tauring introduced me to) is based on this earlier understanding:

> The . . . runecaster uses the [runes] not so much to predict or 'read fortunes' in the popular sense, but rather to engage in sacred play with the signs, to observe the energies signified by the Runes as they 'come into play' in a reading. He or she refines the art of reading the patterns they form in imaginative ways, creating new story lines from ancient materials.

"Creating new story lines from ancient materials"—yes, that speaks to the heart of what I'm doing in connecting with my ancestors. It's probably a good thing that not everyone does genealogy the way I do, because we need people who do painstaking research, who double-check all their data and are careful not to blur the historical record. But I think we need people like me, too, because this idea of sacred play adds a shimmering layer to our speculations about the past. This storytelling and mythmaking, this reading of the runes of our ancestors, helps us weave a tale for ourselves and for our descendants through the blending of imagination, inspiration, and knowledge. In doing so, we can create a new thread in the *öorlog* that's passed on to our descendants.

*This Norwegian family portrait was taken by Knud Knudsen,
one of the first professional photographers in Norway.* (PHOTO
COURTESY OF THE PICTURE COLLECTION, UNIVERSITY OF BERGEN LIBRARY).

8

The Ever-Expanding Web

❖

"There's no way you can be related to Leif Eriksson," said Jerry Paulson, director of the Norwegian American Genealogical Center in Madison, Wisconsin. Seeing my crestfallen expression, he backtracked a bit. "Well, you might be related, but there's no way you can ever prove it."

I knew that claiming ancestry on the basis of a last name shared by hundreds of thousands of Scandinavians likely wouldn't impress a professional genealogist, but hearing it stated so baldly was a bit of a blow. I was glad I hadn't mentioned how I'd wrangled special treatment at L'Anse aux Meadows because of being related to Leif, an experience with parallels to what happened in *National Lampoon's European Vacation* when the Griswolds stayed for several days in the home of a bewildered German couple they mistakenly thought were relatives.

"In genealogy, we're suspicious of anything that can't be documented," Jerry explained. "Lots of people want to claim a connection to the Viking Age, for example—though in my experience most of them want to be a descendant of King Harald Fairhair, not Leif Eriksson. But it's very hard to trace anyone's ancestry back to the Viking Age, because there were almost no records kept in Scandinavia until after it became Christian beginning in the tenth century. It was only then that churches started compiling lists of births, baptisms, marriages, and funerals."

Despite my irritation that anyone would prefer the first king of Norway to the clearly superior Leif Eriksson, I had to admit that Jerry was right in insisting on documentation. Until this point, my own genealogical research had consisted mainly of spitting into a test tube, opening an e-mail from Ancestry.com, and making a lot of imaginative connections between myself and the Vikings. But now it was time to put on my big-girl boots and wade into the part of my gene pool where my quieter, better-behaved relatives were hanging out: the Norwegian immigrants of the nineteenth century.

The Norwegian American Genealogical Center and Naeseth Library was the perfect place to get acquainted with them. Housed in a two-story brick building in downtown Madison, the nonprofit center has its origins in a private collection amassed by Gerhard Naeseth, a University of Wisconsin librarian and scholar of Norwegian-American genealogy and immigrant history. Its shelves are filled with thousands of resources that include emigration documents, Norwegian and Norwegian-American family histories, topographical maps showing the locations of farms and churches in Norway, indexes of names from Norwegian-American cemeteries, and passenger lists from the ships that brought the immigrants to their new home. It is, in short, the mother lode for Scandinavian genealogy.

Realizing that if I hired Jerry Paulson's services to track down all my Norwegian ancestors, the bar tab would quickly exceed my budget, I asked him to focus on just two: Hans and Sila, the great-great-grandparents I'd plucked from my Ancestry.com profile because I liked the sound of their names. I passed a sheet of paper across the table to him that included their birth and death dates and an address of Lærdal, Sogn og Fjordane, an area east of the Norwegian city of Bergen. I was thankful I didn't have to try to pronounce it.

Jerry seemed grateful too as he scanned my notes, though in his case he was probably relieved that I wasn't going to insist he try to trace my lineage to Leif. "I can help you with this," he said. "This is enough to get me started."

For the next hour, as I walked around the library trying to look like I knew what I was doing in a genealogical center, Jerry worked his research magic, pulling books from shelves, checking indexes, flipping through pages, making photocopies, and jotting down notes. Finally he came back to the table where I was sitting. "I found them," he said, a note of quiet satisfaction in his voice. I spared a moment to wonder what the reaction would be to a similar search at an Italian American Genealogical Center. An exchange of hugs? A celebratory glass of vino? No matter. I was just pleased that he'd tracked them down.

The first item Jerry showed me was a photocopy of a parish register from Borgund Church in Sogn og Fjordane. The ornate, handwritten script that filled the page looked indecipherable, but Jerry obviously knew his way around old documents. "Here's Hans," he said, pointing to the second entry. "He was born on November 25, 1815. And I know the place where he was baptized—it's one of the most beautiful stave churches in Norway. I've been there a number of times."

I looked at the record, trying to imagine the small infant who'd grow up to become my great-great grandfather. I pictured a cherubic, blond-haired baby sleeping in the arms of his mother, who looked like one of the gorgeous Norwegian skiers who swoosh down slaloms in the Winter Olympics. As long as I was creating a mental picture of my ancestors, I might as well make them attractive.

Jerry then showed me a page from the Norwegian census of 1801, which someone had thankfully retyped into an easy-to-read chart, assuming, of course, that one can read Norwegian. Jerry traced his finger down the entries until he came to the section detailing the family of Hans's grandfather, who was listed as a *jordløs husmann*. "That meant he was a landless tenant farmer," explained Jerry. "In those days there were two kinds of *husmann*: one had the use of a slip of land for a kitchen garden, and the other kind didn't even have that. Your family was in the second category. It's no wonder they left Norway—there was nothing for them there."

The information fit what I'd been told about my Norwegian relatives while growing up. While no one was interested in doing our family's genealogy back then, I remembered a few vague references to ancestors who were poor farmers in Norway. The only interesting detail was that my mother's paternal grandfather came from a town called Hell, a tidbit that led to considerable snickering from my siblings and me.

Next came information from one of the library's hundreds of local history books known as *bygdebøker* or farm books. These are arguably the most useful resources in the center, the reason that people travel here in person rather than search the Internet or head to the Family History Library in Salt Lake City. The books are so valuable for researchers because of the granular level of detail they offer for rural Norway. Farms there have individual names (some of which date back to the Middle Ages), and these books list who owned the land and often who lived on the property as tenant farmers for many generations.

I was excited when I spotted the words "*Lærdal Kommune*" on its cover. "A commune?" I asked hopefully, imagining my ancestors lounging around a fjord in tie-dye T-shirts smoking weed, or whatever the nineteenth-century Norwegian equivalent was.

"*Kommune* means a municipality," Jerry said, squelching my hopes that my ancestors had been free-spirited hippies. But the information he gleaned from the book was interesting, nevertheless. Flipping back and forth between pages, he showed me the names of several farms where Hans, Sila, and their extended families had lived during the first decades of the nineteenth century.

As we wandered into the thicket of details relating to these relatives, Jerry told me that one of the biggest challenges in Norwegian genealogy is the peculiarities of the country's naming system for many centuries. Children were named after their father, so a John would have sons with a last name of Johnson (or Johnsen) and daughters with a last name of Johnsdatter (meaning daughter). Because it was confusing trying to distinguish between all those Hansens, Olsons, and Larsens, in rural areas people were identified by an additional name that referred to the farm where they lived—for example, Gunhild Larsdatter Sylte lived on the Sylte farm. If they moved (as tenant farmers often did), they'd switch to the name of the new farm, which meant that people could have multiple names during the course of their lives. Gunhild Larsdatter Sylte could become Gunhild Larsdatter Snarhol just by moving a couple of miles.

As you can imagine, this last name promiscuity tends to make genealogy researchers use swear words not generally heard in the hushed confines of libraries. It wasn't until 1923 that Norway finally said enough is enough and passed a law that required everyone to have a hereditary last name. "The naming issue is the single biggest stumbling block people have in searching for their Norwegian ancestors," Jerry said, which made me realize that the $40 per hour I was paying him was well worth the money.

Finally, Jerry showed me a book that pinpointed the year when Hans and Sila had had enough, when the poverty and hard work and lack of prospects in their homeland made them put all their chips on the roulette wheel of emigration: whatever America might offer them was likely better than what Norway could provide. In 1850 they packed their belongings and said goodbye to everyone in Lærdal, all their relatives and friends and neighbors, the people who'd been their entire world since their births, and traveled to Bergen, where they boarded a ship named the *Ørnen*.

I remembered my earlier curiosity about whether they'd known each other before coming to this country, back when I first spotted their names on Ancestry.com. My answer came when I saw their names listed as the twelfth and thirteenth passengers on the ship, which arrived in New York on July 15, 1850—the middle of summer, likely much warmer than what they were used to in the north. Hans was thirty-six; Sila was twenty-three. In my mind's eye I saw them stepping off the boat in New York Harbor, their legs wobbly from weeks at sea, taking in the cacophony of sounds and sights with wide eyes. They would never see the land of their birth again.

WHAT THEY LEFT BEHIND

Today, if you want to immigrate to Norway, all I can say is "Good luck with that." As one of the most desirable places to live on earth, Norway can be extremely picky about who it accepts as citizens. But in the nineteenth century, the country was shedding citizens so fast that only Ireland lost a greater percentage of its population to emigration. The reason was that life in Norway was exceedingly hard for many of its citizens, especially if you were a day laborer, tenant farmer, servant, or pauper—groups that included about half of its population.

Hans and Sila were the first of my relatives to make the journey from Norway to America, but over the next four decades, they were joined by Johan, Tore, Karen, Ingeborg, Brita, Anna, Carrie, and the Andrews (there were two of them). Some came from the heart of the fjord region, as Hans and Sila did, though it's unlikely they ever knew each other because they emigrated in different decades. Others lived near Oslo, and another set hailed from near the northern city of Trondheim. Most were unmarried and in their twenties when they left. Then and now, emigration is often a decision made by the restless, the unattached, and the ambitious.

Since only 4 percent of land in Norway is arable, the country has always been a tough place to make a living. In the nineteenth century, economic pressure increased due to a surge in population, likely because of small-pox vaccinations and the introduction of the potato, which improved nutrition for the poorest classes. Farms were subdivided into smaller and smaller plots, making it even harder to grow enough food to feed the larger families.

The sorry state of medical care added to the misery. Physicians rarely ventured into the remote parts of the country, and even when they did, their knowledge and skills were limited and sometimes harmful. Self-trained folk healers and midwives dealt with some medical conditions pretty well, but many people suffered and died from illnesses that would be easily treatable today. Childbirth was perilous for both mother and baby, and diseases such as cholera and typhoid fever periodically swept through communities, leaving devastation behind.

One of the most pernicious diseases was rickets, which is caused by a lack of vitamin D. Before it was discovered that cod liver oil could make up for the low levels of sunlight during the long Scandinavian winters, rickets was common. Healthy babies would mysteriously sicken, their joints swelling and bones softening. People called them changelings because it was believed the *huldrefolk*, the hidden people, had come in the night and switched the human baby for one of theirs.

Jerry Paulson was right about Hans and Sila—there was nothing for them in Norway. Except, of course, their loved ones and all they'd ever known.

The first boatload of Norwegians, a group of fifty-two religious dissenters, arrived in New York in 1825 on the *Restauration*. During the next decades the flow of emigrants from Norway was just a trickle, but by 1850, the year Hans and Sila stepped on board the ship in Bergen, the numbers were beginning to swell into the thousands each year. Between 1820 and 1920, nearly a million people from Norway emigrated to the United States, most under thirty years of age and from rural areas.

The Norwegians called it "America Fever," a contagion that spread throughout the country thanks to letters sent back home by those who'd left. The epistles were copied and passed from person to person and often published in newspapers. Many of the correspondents extolled the economic opportunities of their new home, downplaying the hardships they endured and giving practical advice on how others could follow their example. "I in no way wish to return," wrote Ole K. Trovatten in

1842. "Any poor person who will work diligently can become a well-to-do man here in a short time."

In the early decades of immigration, most Norwegians had to travel to another country to board a boat sailing to America, leaving from ports that included Liverpool in England, LeHavre in France, Hamburg in Germany, and Gothenburg in Sweden. Before the 1860s, the sea journey was long, dangerous, and miserable. Sailing ships took at least six weeks to cross the Atlantic, with the passengers packed together below deck in unsanitary conditions that bred illness and often led to death. The invention of the steamship shortened the voyage to about thirteen days, but it was still far more arduous than the journeys of today. Many people traveled on pre-paid tickets sent to them by relatives and friends in America, with the expectation that they would work off the cost of their trip after they arrived—usually a full year of work.

There were only two periods in Norwegian history when its people left in great numbers: the Viking Age and the immigrant era. In both periods, the primary lure was greater economic opportunities abroad. But while the Vikings came with swords, their nineteenth-century descendants traveled with a few meager belongings packed into trunks. When people saw them approaching by boat, I doubt anyone was scared in the least.

GENEALOGY 101

My experience in Madison gave me a primer in how to do genealogy the way it's been done for centuries, as opposed to spitting into a test tube and clicking on computer links. I learned that no matter what your ethnic background is, the search for family roots begins with one person: you. Go ahead—take a piece of paper, and write down your name and the date and place you were born. Then add your parents' information. Congratulations! You're doing genealogy!

At this point you might be able to keep climbing your family tree easily. Maybe your clan is full of storytellers and record keepers, with people who have files full of detailed and accurate genealogical information they're happy to share and aunts who write down the charming stories about Grandma's growing up years on the farm. At family reunions perhaps you and your second cousins pore over old photographs so you can figure out who's that guy in the bowler hat standing next to Great Uncle Theodore, the one who deserted the Prussian army and ended up owning a haberdashery shop in Buffalo, New York.

Most of us, alas, do not come from families like this. Genealogy for African Americans, in particular, can be fraught because they have the challenge of tracing ancestors robbed of their history through slavery and of finding white ancestors who are likely on their family tree because of rape. Or you may be adopted with no information about your birth parents, or your relatives may be uninterested or suspicious of your efforts ("Why do you want to know Dad's birthdate? Is this a scam?"). Family photos pile up in boxes and eventually get thrown away because no one has a clue who is pictured in them. Your cousin might have done some genealogical research, but it turns out she entered the wrong data into a family-search website and most of her information is about a set of people you're not actually related to.

But your journey into the past can begin with even a tiny scrap of information—and because history is a big place, it helps to have a plan before you set out exploring. Think about what intrigues you the most about your family history. Maybe it's finding information about your great grandparents, or the relative who died in a bar fight during the California gold rush, or the one who came west on an Orphan Train in the 1880s. You may never end up with a family tree that's the size of a redwood, but you can still learn about a few individual lives and the eras that shaped them.

In sifting through potential sources of information, keep in mind that not all historical records are created equal. The most reliable are those recorded close to the time the event occurred, including birth, marriage, and death certificates; diplomas; and legal deeds. Information from obituaries, newspaper articles, military records, census records, and family histories are considered less reliable. These secondary sources should be verified by primary sources whenever possible, because the further away you get away from the actual event, the more likely mistakes were made.

It's also important to keep a record of your research trail so that you don't have to go back and repeat what you've already done. Take pictures of old photographs and records so that you have your own copies. Genealogical software can be very useful, helping you keep track of what you've learned as well as allowing you to link with online records and other people's family trees. Remember that you're creating a set of resources not only for yourself, but also for relatives who might later pick up the search, including your own descendants.

One of the most valuable things we can do is collect the stories of our family elders before it's too late. Were their parents wealthy or poor or somewhere in between? What did they do for fun as children? What occupations did their parents and grandparents have? How did they celebrate holidays? What were their schools like? If possible, make an audio or video recording of the interview. While you're at it, ask them to help you identify the people in those old photos stuffed into boxes (an added bonus is that the pictures can often jog their memories).

While genealogy has become easier than ever before thanks to the Internet, my experience with Jerry Paulson shows that consulting an expert can help you quickly cut through historical tangles. A good way to find one is by joining a genealogy society (before I left the library that afternoon, I filled out a form to become a member of the Norwegian American Genealogical Center). Whether you're a Mennonite, a New Englander, an African American from Ohio, or a descendent of Daniel Boone, there's a group waiting for you. Associations may have specialized resources you can't find online and offer classes, workshops, and conventions, giving you access to a cadre of people who can help you when you hit a dead end (a common problem while researching dead people). These activities turn your genealogical quest into a social outlet, further adding to the enjoyment. Your new buddies don't have to be in your part of the country; many genealogy buffs connect solely online.

For many people, part of the fun is the difficulty of finding information about generations before them. Every new clue gets treasured because so few of them exist. And like gambling, one of the attractions of genealogy is random reinforcement—you never know when you're going to find something valuable, and those "aha" moments can become addictive.

All of this makes me wonder what genealogy will be like for our descendants. Given the millions of people searching for information today, will there be anything left to discover in the future? At a certain point, maybe the historical record can't be squeezed any harder. But once the genealogists start looking into our generation, they'll confront the opposite challenge: a fire hose spouting too much information. Imagine looking over the shoulder of your great-great granddaughter who's researching you. Think of the digital record you've created in your years on earth, the social media posts, financial transactions, and multiple jobs and homes. The problem won't be finding information but instead sifting through too much of it. If we know what our ancestors ate on any given day, when they went shopping for a new pair of shoes, or what meme they forwarded to all of their friends, how can we decide what's important?

Despite the deluge of information, our descendants might nevertheless find it hard to decipher our spiritual beliefs, given the scattershot nature of our digital fingerprints. They'll have more to go on than a baptism recorded in spidery handwriting in an old ledger, but even with online oversharing, people's inner lives often remain a mystery. Genealogists of the future will likely still wonder about the spiritual musings and inclinations of their ancestors (except my descendants, of course, who will instead have the fire-hose problem).

I was surprised to learn that the steady stream of people visiting the Norwegian American Genealogy Center includes actual Norwegians. I'd assumed that the only people interested in its information would be the people on this side of the Atlantic. "A lot of Norwegians are curious about what happened to their relatives who emigrated," explained Jerry. "They come here trying to track down the rest of the story, to learn what happened to Great Uncle Olaf after he left Norway and was never heard from again. This is a part of the immigration story that we often don't think much about—the people who were left behind."

I asked Jerry if people are often surprised by what they find. "Oh, yes," he said. "A lot of people are shocked to find illegitimate children among their ancestors, for example, though why that should be surprising, I don't know."

Having a child out of wedlock wasn't that uncommon in nineteenth-century Norway, Jerry explained. Many landless people slept communally in barns, and courting couples often practiced "bundling," which meant they slept together but were supposed to be fully clothed. Both situations, not surprisingly, led to unexpected pregnancies. Churches recorded these births alongside those of parents who were married, but with a special designation indicating the circumstances of their births.

His words prompted me to flip through my notes to confirm something I'd nearly forgotten: Hans had a child out of marriage, at least according to a family tree I'd linked to on Ancestry.com. I showed Jerry the meager information I'd jotted down about her: Anna Hansdatter Lysne, born in 1840. "She was ten years old when Hans left for America," I told him. "Can you find any information on what happened to her?"

He set off to the stacks once again, but this time the search wasn't as successful as before. "It's curious," he said when he returned. "I keep running into a brick wall with this. Let me do some more work on my own. I'll get back to you with what I find out." He looked excited, and I realized that for a professional genealogist, mysteries like these are part of the reason they'd gotten into the business. The thrill was the hunt, not just the end result.

As for me, I drove home to Iowa City with much to ponder. I thought of Hans and Sila and their voyage across the

Atlantic, wondering whether they'd gotten sick or encountered storms, and about all my other Norwegian relatives who'd left their homeland. I speculated on what had been the final straw that made them leave, whether it was a failed potato crop, a dishonest landlord, or their little brother getting swapped out for a changeling. While the Vikings inspired me with their tales of bravery and exploration, these nineteenth-century relatives impressed me with their grit. They weren't flashy, and no one was making TV dramas about their adventures or trying to emulate their fashion choices, but like the Vikings, they had courage and determination.

And I thought about the daughter that Hans had left behind, whether he'd ever sent money to help pay for her support and whether she'd dreamed of following him to America. I wondered if her descendants had ever shown up at the Norwegian American Genealogical Center, searching for what happened to Hans.

THE WEB WOVEN AT OUR BIRTHS

As I dove deeper into my research about my nineteenth-century relatives, the Norse concept of *öorlog* kept returning to me. According to Kari Tauring, *öorlog* can be thought of as a combination of our DNA, ancestral karma, and inherited conditions, plus the accumulation of our actions, words, and intentions in our present lifetimes. "You can think of your *öorlog* as your particular corner of the Web of Wyrd," she told me. "When we explore our *öorlog*, we can better understand the influences and forces shaping our lives today."

The concepts of *wyrd* and *öorlog* put a new spin on searching for family roots. While at one level genealogy is about compiling names and dates and documents, the filling in of family trees and the connecting with second cousins once removed, perhaps there's a deeper process at work as well. Maybe our souls need these tendrils of connection to the past, to our *öorlog*, in order for us to flourish—and one of the reasons that so many people have fragmented souls today is that these ties of connection have been severed.

I was intrigued, too, by the ways in which *öorlog* related to my musings about spiritual DNA. I'd latched onto the concept because I resisted the idea that my identity is limited solely to my genetic heritage and individual choices: spiritual DNA became my way of imagining the larger forces that shape who I am. *Öorlog* added new layers to that understanding. I imagined the Norns at my birth, seeing them perched just below the ceiling of my mother's hospital room. I watched as they first spun and measured out the thread of my life and then added it to an infinitely large afghan they've been knitting for millennia.

Öorlog is also related to how important ancestors were to the Norse. After being buried with the goods they'd need after death, from swords and horses to boats, they lived on in Valhalla or other corners of the nine realms. People made sacrifices to them, went to the places they were buried to consult with them, and honored them in hopes they would bless their descendants with prosperity and good fortune. It was believed that the dead could even be reborn within the family line.

Put aside for a moment, please, the dismaying thought that your cantankerous grandfather might be reborn as your grandchild. Instead imagine what it would be like to live in a world where the boundaries between life and death are fluid, one in which you're embedded in an immense web that influences you in countless ways, created by the choices of people long dead as well as your own actions. I thought of the family tree that I'd stared at many times on my computer screen, with its branches and subbranches that extended farther each time I clicked on a link. At any one moment I could see only a small fraction of these connections, but I could now imagine them extending far beyond the computer screen, connecting me to lives far away and ages long past.

If there is such a thing as *öorlog*, then for many people it's full of trauma, of course—those whose ancestors suffered from pogroms, genocide, war, starvation, and brutality far worse than what my nineteenth-century Norwegian relatives had to endure. One choice is to simply sever this psychic thread of connection, to ignore all that came before. But starting afresh can be much harder than it seems, and inherited grief has a way of resurfacing in our lives. Some of the transmission is biological—poor prenatal nutrition, for example, can affect DNA. And some of it gets passed down through patterns of behavior. Therapists say that it can take multiple generations for the trauma caused by alcoholism or sexual abuse, for example, to be fully healed so that the descendants no longer have to bear the burden of dysfunction.

We can think of this in purely physical and psychological terms, but I found that the concept of *öorlog* gave me a useful new way of looking at this phenomenon. Kari Tauring, in fact, believes that we can send healing back in time. "Many people walk around with fractured souls, not realizing how their *öorlog* is shaping them," she said. "Through ritual work and prayer we can find and mend those fragments. Our ancestors are waiting for the healing we can offer them, and our descendants are counting on us to lay healthy patterns for them. It's about unrolling the threads that were spun before us and finding out which parts of the thread were spun too thin and which were grafted onto something that we really don't want to add to the future. We can set a new pattern in the weave for our descendants to follow."

These notions can seem pretty strange in a culture such as ours that so highly prizes individualism. We glory in starting afresh, in pretending like we're creating everything for the first time. But those who love genealogy, who have a deep respect for those who have come before, may have an intuitive sense for the power of *öorlog*.

Perhaps part of the pleasure we feel in genealogy is our ancestors' pleasure in being remembered. As we research their lives, sing their songs, eat their traditional foods, and carry on their customs (well, at least the benign ones, not the raiding and pillaging), they get the chance to live again in us, even if Grandpa isn't reborn as our grandson. I thought of the way that Gudrid's story called to me, enticing me to learn more about her and the Viking Age, and how the Web of Wyrd now connected me to Hans and Sila and Hans's daughter Anna. I realized how much my sense of identity was changing as a result of my search for ancestors. I now saw my life on a much larger scale, one that put my individual life and its struggles into greater perspective. And the more I learned about the stories of my ancestors, the more I sensed that at some level they were pleased by the attention.

Nordic Dancers perform in front of Vesterheim in Decorah,
Iowa, during the town's annual Nordic Fest celebration.

9

Time Capsules of the Past

-:✳:-

I'd driven the streets of Decorah, the small Iowa town where I'd grown up, thousands of times, but until I started exploring my ancestry I'd never noticed the irony of the real estate signs posted on many of its front lawns: Viking Realtors. Think about it: would you really want the *Vikings* in charge of your house sale? When they arrived at your house to estimate its value, they'd probably steal things when you weren't looking, grabbing a necklace or two from the upstairs bedroom and peeking into drawers for loose cash. I expect title searches wouldn't get done properly, either, given their disregard for legal formalities. And when it came time to close the sale, how could you be sure they wouldn't just pocket the money and then move into the house themselves?

Viking Realtors is just one of many Scandinavian-themed establishments in my hometown, from Viking State Bank to Vesterheim, the National Norwegian-American Museum and Heritage Center. Settled by Norwegian immigrants in the 1850s, the town has had a distinctly Norwegian lilt to its identity ever since. Images of Norse trolls peak out from many windows, Norwegian flags hang on people's front porches, and Nordic Fest celebrates all things Scandinavian every summer.

Growing up on a farm ten miles away, I went to school in Decorah and after graduation attended Luther College, which was founded by the Norwegian Evangelical Lutheran Church in America in 1861. Though I was steeped in Norwegian traditions from a young age, that didn't mean I was very enthusiastic about them—in fact, I viewed the town's Norwegian rah-rah with a slightly jaundiced eye. My last name was nothing special in this community where Ericksons, Olsons, Johnsons, and Petersons filled page after page in the phone book. Besides, the town was full of much more authentic Scandinavians than me. These professional Norwegians, as I dubbed them, wore folk costumes without embarrassment, knitted wool sweaters that wouldn't seem out of place on a ski slope in Lillehammer, and proudly displayed trunks in their living rooms that had been hauled across the Atlantic by their great grandparents. They could sing the Norwegian national anthem word for word and had pictures on their walls of themselves posing next to attractive Norwegian cousins. As for me, I was more of a Jack Norwegian, the Lutheran equivalent of those Jack Mormons who didn't want to take on the hard parts of their religion.

But Kari Tauring's comments about *öorlog*—the web that connects us to our ancestors—made me realize there was a lot I didn't know about my roots in Decorah. It was time to go back and look at it from an adult's perspective, to reevaluate my relationship with this capital of Norwegian culture in America.

As I began making plans to do so, there was something that needed doing: I sat down at a table, put on a bib, and dished myself up a large helping of humble pie—because I realized I'd become one of those Norwegian boosters who'd so irritated me growing up.

It's not surprising that the United States, a nation of immigrants, has many communities that cherish their ethnic origins. From Polish and Pakistani to Puerto Rican, the country is full of enclaves where the foods, crafts, languages, and traditions of other countries flourish. In Mexican neighborhoods, Day of the Dead is celebrated, while the Irish have St. Patrick's Day, and the Swedes, St. Lucia's Day. Montpelier, Vermont, preserves its French connections; Solvang, California, its Danish ones. Dearborn, Michigan, which is home to the largest Arab American community in America, has some of the best Middle Eastern food this side of Baghdad as well as the impressive Arab American National Museum.

What makes one community cling to its origins and another leave them behind is a curious thing. Sometimes outside influences play a large role. During World War I, many German-American neighborhoods downplayed their identity because of anti-German sentiment. In other places, demographic changes fray cultural ties, as outsiders move in and insiders move out. Chinatowns gradually become Cuban, then Filipino, and then a mix of ethnicities, though hopefully retaining at least a few restaurants run by the children and grandchildren of the previous waves of immigrants (food, after all, is usually the last ethnic affiliation to be left behind).

Some places, however, like Decorah, remain strongly identified with their ethnic origins, even after more than a century. Part of the reason might be similar to my own identification with Leif Eriksson: you go with what you have. Cherishing your Dutch or Greek or Laotian ties sets you apart from other neighborhoods or towns and can give you a greater sense of community. Ethnic customs can attract tourism dollars, too, thanks to their distinctive festivals, stores, and restaurants. If the traditions are strong enough, they can draw in new residents as well, people who are willing to go along with the community zeitgeist even though they know they look ridiculous in lederhosen at Oktoberfest.

Those of us who grew up in communities with strong ethnic identifications have, in a sense, dual passports. Even after we move away, many of us still have one foot in that other culture—though sometimes the connection can take the form of rebellion rather than appreciation (full confession: as a child I used to call Nordic Fest "Nordic Fester").

Having swallowed the final bite of humble pie, my *öor-log* journey to Decorah took me first to Vesterheim. This museum, whose name means Home in the West, houses the most extensive collection of Norwegian-American artifacts in the world. While I'd visited it several times growing up, mostly what I remembered were boring displays of nineteenth-century antiques, rough-hewn pioneer-era buildings, and making faces behind our teacher's back on field trips.

As I toured its handsome, three-story, brick building and surrounding complex of a dozen historic structures as an adult, however, my first impression was that either Vesterheim had changed, or I had. While there were still old-fashioned displays of artifacts brought over from the Old Country and exhibits showing the hardscrabble life of the early immigrants, the museum seemed much more engaging, not just an homage to the past but also a reflection on how Nordic traditions continue to be part of America today. That's especially true in the museum's Folk Art School, which has instructors from around the United States as well as Norway teaching courses ranging from woodworking and weaving to the decorative painting known as rosemaling, the floral designs that adorn nearly everything in Norwegian-American culture (the museum even displays a refrigerator door covered with rosemaling).

Though I was tempted by a class on hand-forged knife blades—a good thing to have the next time I hung around with Viking reenactors—instead I signed up for a course in the making of *rømmegrøt*, a word that sounds like someone is trying to stifle a burp but actually is a type of cream porridge. I remembered eating it as a child at church dinners and was curious what an entire class on it would be like. Our group of a half-dozen people gathered in the basement of the Bethania Lutheran Church, a rural North Dakota structure that was moved to the museum grounds in 1992. Our teacher, Darlene Fossum-Martin, began by explaining the significance of porridge in Norwegian life before and after the pre-Industrial Era.

"Porridge formed the basis of most rural people's diets," she said. "It was usually made with coarsely ground grain mixed with water or milk. But for special occasions like Christmas they made *rømmegrøt*, which is a thicker porridge made with finely ground flour, sour cream, sugar, and butter. They'd make an extra bowl to put outside as an offering to the *nisse*, the elves that were said to watch over houses and farms. It was also brought as a gift to new mothers to help them recover from childbirth."

As we assembled the ingredients and stirred the thick mixture in a big pot on the stove, I reflected on what it would be like to have ancestors who'd known the joys of garlic, spicy peppers, and aromatic spices. Still, the finished product was rich and comforting, especially with some cinnamon and sugar sprinkled on top followed by a generous amount of melted butter. As I ate, I thought of my ancestors for whom this was a treasured delicacy. I felt a twinge of guilt when I remembered all the times I'd complained about the blandness of Norwegian-American cuisine. Given how hard it was to live in their harsh northern climate, they did the best with what they had.

"More than any other single thing, foods maintain ties to ethnicity," said Darlene. "They help immigrants cope with homesickness, and later generations associate them with their childhood and special occasions, which give the dishes another set of positive associations. Recipes carry history."

Later, during a chat with chief curator Laurann Gilbertson, I learned more about how Decorah came to be so prominent in the Norwegian exodus. "A lot of it was just a historical accident," she said. "The town was originally settled by a small group of English settlers, but then in the 1850s some Norwegians came, and then more, and then some more. That's how immigration works—people want to live where there are people like them. Along with Dane County in Wisconsin, Decorah became a mother colony, a place where Norwegians knew they could find other Norwegians. And because these people tended to marry fellow Norwegians, even in subsequent generations, that ethnic identification continued." (And that's how I ended up being one of the least ethnically diverse individuals in the United States, I mentally added.)

When I asked how that identification continues today in Decorah, Laurann mentioned food traditions, from church *lutefisk* dinners at Christmas to the ubiquitous potato *lefse*, a kind of soft flatbread. In addition, a large number of its residents have been to Norway—it's practically the Holy Land for people from Decorah, she said—while Scandinavian first names are popular for children. I pictured kindergarten classes full of Bjorns, Pers, Astrids, and Einars, though I doubted Thor has made much of a comeback, let alone Snorri. "People here still tend to be more aware of their ethnic heritage than in many places," Laurann said.

When I asked what real Norwegians think about the museum when they visit, she admitted that some of them are disappointed. "They say it's too much about the past and not enough about contemporary Norway," Laurann said. "But we only have so much space and resources, and our job is to focus on the immigrant Norwegian-American experience and its continuing threads today in this country."

I realized the truth of her words when I remembered visiting Pella, an Iowa town that celebrates its Dutch origins, where I was amused by how different its prim and proper vibe was from contemporary Amsterdam, with its Red Light District and smell of marijuana wafting from coffee shops. Many communities with strong ethnic identities are time capsules of what their mother countries were like when their ancestors left as immigrants, celebrating the customs and language of much earlier eras.

Before I left the museum, I toured a temporary exhibition of pictures by Knud Knudsen, who established one of Norway's first photography businesses in the city of Bergen in 1864 and traveled frequently to fjord country to record the lives of the people living there. I looked at several dozen of his black-and-white photos with interest. The faces of the people in the pictures were familiar to me, these men with their square jaws and resolute expressions, and sturdy women who looked like they could make *rømmegrøt* with one hand tied behind their back. They stood in front of tiny huts that had goats eating off their grass roofs and posed next to carts filled with belongings, headed to the ships that would bring them across the Atlantic to America. These were my people, separated from me only by time.

Two photos in particular made an impression on me. The first was of several people working in a tiny field set at a 45-degree angle on the side of a fjord, the women using hoes while a man walks behind a pony-sized horse. Across the fjord looms a snow-capped mountain. The second photo was taken by Knudsen on a visit to his relatives in the town of Thor, Iowa, in 1893. The land is flat as a pancake, with only a few small trees in the distance to vary the monotony. There's a two-story, white house and large barn on the property, surrounded by a picket fence, while a herd of fat cattle grazes in the foreground.

The first picture has stunning natural beauty, a stark contrast to the ho-hum setting of the farmstead in Iowa. But as Knudsen's relatives knew very well, you can't eat scenery.

A NEW HOME IN THE WEST

Hans and Sila were among the first wave of Norwegian settlers in Decorah, according to Midge Kjome of the Decorah Genealogy Association. (Having grown up in Decorah, I knew without being told that her last name is pronounced *cho-me*.) She was happy to help me track down information on what happened to my great-great-grandparents after they'd landed in New York in July of 1850.

"They first made their way to Racine County, Wisconsin, where they were married in October of that same year," she told me. "In 1852 they came to the Decorah area and settled in Glenwood Township ten miles east of town. Hans bought his first piece of land in January of 1856, another parcel two months later, and a third in 1867. He ended up with about two hundred acres, which made him among the more prosperous farmers in the township."

Opening up a large, leather-bound ledger, she showed me his land transactions, each recorded in an ornate cursive hand, and then pointed out the location of his farm on a map from an 1874 plat book. I realized that it was on the same country road where my mother had grown up, just a few miles from the farm where I was raised. After my ancestors' great leap across the Atlantic, their descendants stayed put for several generations, and it was only in my generation that wanderlust has struck again. I felt a twinge of regret when I realized that with the recent death of my ninety-year-old mother, my family's nearly 170-year tenure in Decorah has ended. Given the nomadic nature of contemporary society, there's a good chance none of my descendants will ever beat that record in any other place.

I knew from my own reading the general outlines of Norwegian immigration in the mid-nineteenth century. While later immigrants typically landed in Quebec, Hans and Sila were part of an earlier wave who passed through New York (though this was several decades before Ellis Island came into operation, the city was still a popular entry point). From New York they likely traveled to the middle of the country by a combination of rail, steamer, canal boat, and walking, a journey of nearly a thousand miles. It made sense that they'd first gone to Racine County, Midge said, where there was a sizeable Norwegian settlement.

Two years later they traveled for unknown reasons farther west to Decorah, a town that had been founded just three years before they arrived. The indigenous people of the region, the Winnebago, had been resettled in Minnesota by the federal government in 1848, though there were some Native Americans who periodically passed through the area, and white settlers would sometimes find their hidden caches of food, an indication that they'd hoped to return. Hans had likely earned money by taking whatever jobs he could find, probably farming or logging, gradually accumulating the cash he needed to buy land of his own. The Homestead Act, which gave 160 acres of land to settlers willing to settle on the property and farm it, wouldn't come into existence until 1862, so he had to buy his farm outright.

"Those early immigrants tended to stay to themselves in rural Decorah," Midge told me. "They spoke Norwegian among themselves and had a tight community. It wasn't until the second generation that they started coming more into town, because they knew their children needed better English skills."

Hans and Sila largely faded from the historical record after those land purchases, showing up in census records but otherwise not making much of a ripple in local history. Sila gave birth to eight children, six of whom survived to adulthood, including my great-grandmother Berthe. After Hans died in 1890, Sila was a widow for fourteen years before dying at the age of seventy-six. "She was a kind and loving wife and mother, and will be mourned by a large circle of friends," reads her obituary, a barebones recounting of her life that makes me hungry for more details.

Recalling how Kari Tauring can name a lineage of female ancestors dating back to the seventeenth century, I mentally listed some of my own: Grace, Alma, Carrie, Ingeborg, Berthe, Brita, Anna, and Sila. There were many more, of course, but my genealogical research had given me the outlines, at least, of the lives of these women—where they lived, who they married, how many children they'd raised, and how many they'd buried as infants or small children. I found it ironic that I knew so much more about Gudrid, who lived a thousand years ago, than many of them. But I knew enough to claim these women as kin and to see the faint glimmer of their threads woven into my own *öorlog* corner of the Web of Wyrd.

DIVIDED HEARTS

My ancestors were among the nearly 800,000 Norwegians who settled in the upper Midwest between 1850 and 1910, creating a stronghold of Scandinavian culture that continues to this day. Minnesota has the largest number of residents of Norwegian descent, followed by Wisconsin, while North Dakota has the most per capita (about 30 percent of its citizens). In the United States, the number of people who claim Norwegian ancestry is about 4.6 million, just a little less than the current population of Norway at 5.4 million.

The Norwegians tended to do well in their new homeland. Many were used to living in isolated rural areas with harsh weather, so the rigors of life on the windswept prairies of the upper Midwest weren't entirely unfamiliar. The Norwegian Americans remained farmers longer than other nineteenth-century immigrant groups, even into the second, third, and fourth generations. Perhaps it was because they came from a country where arable land was so scarce: once they owned good farmland of their own, they didn't want to let it go.

Still, life was hard, especially for the women, who tended to be more socially isolated than the men, as well as weighed down by the endless duties of child rearing, housework, and farm chores. In 1870, one third of children died before they were ten, so it would have been a lucky woman indeed who succeeded in raising all her children to adulthood without at least one premature death. They endured trials that included prairie fires, fierce blizzards, and grasshopper infestations that ate the crops. But gradually life improved as their husbands learned how to farm in the new land, larger houses were built, and the railroads and improved roads helped ease their social isolation.

What didn't change for many of them, though, was a divided heart, something that they shared with immigrants of all eras. No matter how much their prospects had improved in the new land, their thoughts often drifted home. "We have it good, but America is not Norway," wrote an immigrant in a letter from the 1850s. "There is always something strange and unfamiliar about everything here."

Reading about the lives of these immigrants, I could see why some tried to create a Little Norway in Decorah, a corner of northeast Iowa whose forested hills, limestone bluffs, and clear streams must have made it seem a little more like their homeland than other parts of the Midwest. The town's Luther

College became a center for the training of pastors as well as the sons of the pioneers (it wasn't until 1936 that the school became coeducational). The *Decorah-Posten*, a Norwegian language newspaper, was published here from 1874 to 1972, making it the longest-lasting Norwegian-language newspaper in North America. At its height it had a circulation of 45,000 readers from all over the United States and Norway.

I knew from my growing-up years that the ties between Decorah and Norway remained strong long after the original immigrants had died. I remembered the excitement when members of the Norwegian royal family visited the town, and how Luther College hosted groups of actual Norwegians, not just Norwegian Americans, for cultural programs each summer. One year, one of these Norwegians scandalized the locals when she stripped down to her undies in a laundromat and blithely walked around while the rest of her wardrobe was being washed and dried. People concluded that she was practical but not very modest.

It's the town's annual Nordic Fest, however, that most lionizes Decorah's ethnic origins. This extravaganza of Scandinavian foods, dance, music, crafts, storytelling, and customs draws 10,000 people on a late July weekend that almost always has weather that's closer to that of Mississippi than Norway. No matter: during Nordic Fest, Decorah becomes a Little Norway, and everyone is at least a little bit Norwegian. And as I deepened my search for roots, I knew I needed to experience it again as an adult, without any teenage snarkiness.

Wandering through the Nordic Fest crowds on a sunny July morning, that wasn't hard, as I quickly got caught up in the sheer wholesomeness of it. Many people wore Norwegian-inspired dress, from the expensive, ornately embroidered folk dresses known as *bunads* to a simplified version of the traditional national costume (black skirts, white aprons, and red bodices for women; vests and knickers for men). Blond-haired mothers pushed strollers containing toddlers waving Norwegian flags, and the roped-off main street was lined with food booths selling delicacies such as *krumkake, kringla,* and *lefse.*

In the Saturday morning parade, I watched as float after float passed by displaying Decorah's connections to its ethnic roots, from the Luren Singers (the oldest Norwegian-American chorus in the world) to ones bearing friendly looking Viking warriors waving plastic swords. People dressed up as trolls sprinted along beside the floats and threw candy at the crowd, while the Nordic Dancers, a group of costumed young people, stopped to entertain us with quick snippets of folk dances.

After the parade, I wandered through an encampment of Vikings who'd set up tents near Vesterheim, recalling my time among the reenactors in Moorhead. In between visiting politely with visitors, they staged mock attacks, yelling at the top of their lungs and banging their weapons as they charged across the grass, only to stop short in front of shrieking children and wide-eyed adults.

In the afternoon I attended a performance of *Farvel Du Moder Norge* (Farewell to Mother Norway), a musical about the emigration to America from the perspective of those left behind. Performed by a choir from Norway, it was surprisingly moving, in part because I hadn't thought much about what it was like to be the ones left behind in the Old Country. One of the songs, especially, was haunting—a tune about a mother watching the ship leave port with her son on board. She waves him goodbye, praying to God for a safe voyage, and I wondered about Hans and Sila's final farewell to their parents, each knowing they were unlikely to ever see their loved ones again.

A song named "*Husmannen*" struck me as well. I recognized the term from my visit to the genealogical society in Madison: a *husmann* was a sharecropper, also known as a cotter. According to the song's description in the program, "Being a cotter meant being a second-rate citizen, not owning land, barely making a living." As the choir performed the tune, I reflected on the fact that Hans, who was penniless when he left Norway in 1850, bought property just six years later. For him, at least, the letters sent back home by enthusiastic new immigrants had spoken the truth.

Later that evening, I sat on a bench in the downtown, listening to a performance of a couple of fiddlers and savoring the coolness of the air after the heat of the day. The audience in front of me looked like a Norman Rockwell painting, with white-haired ladies chatting with each other and children snuggled in the laps of their parents. Then on the sidewalk behind them I spotted a Viking, a man I recognized from the reenactors encampment. Tall, well-muscled, and handsome, he wore a tunic with a dagger at his waist and was licking an ice cream cone as he strolled.

I smiled, a bit ruefully, as I realized that the scene summed up for me some of my ambivalence about my hometown. I both admired and regretted the fact that Decorah has found a way to domesticate its ethnic heritage. It seemed to me as if only the picturesque and charming parts had been kept, while the shadow side that gave it added depth and meaning—including the violence of the Vikings and the harshness of the immigrant era—had been tucked into a rosemaled trunk in the attic.

FAMILY SPIRITS

Before leaving Decorah that weekend, I wanted to visit the farm where Hans and Sila had lived. I drove ten miles outside of town, turned down a dusty gravel road, and then inched along slowly, frequently consulting a photocopy of a page from the 1874 plat book, mentally comparing it to what I saw before me. At last I came to a spot that seemed right, or at least was in the same vicinity. After getting out of my car, I looked with appreciation at its patchwork landscape of woods interspersed with corn and soybean fields, all framed by a blue sky with fluffy clouds. It was idyllic, yet I suddenly felt hesitant about being there, realizing how little actually connected me to this spot of land that had passed out of my family generations ago.

I could see that it certainly wasn't the best farmland—hilly rather than flat, it would be difficult to plow. I recalled reading that the early Norwegian immigrants often bypassed the open prairie and chose instead to settle near streams and rivers, places with trees for building materials and fuel but less suitable for farming. They must have felt a little more at home surrounded by trees, these people who'd grown up among the thick forests of Norway. It was only later that the immigrants realized how fertile the Midwestern grasslands were, once the thick roots of the prairie were broken by the steel plow.

Hans and Sila's first house was almost certainly built of logs, likely a single room with an upstairs loft. I hoped they'd moved into a larger place, or at least expanded that simple cabin, before all of their six kids arrived on the scene. With a horse and wagon, it would have taken them several hours to travel into Decorah, not a journey they'd make lightly or often. I wondered if they were happy to be settled after their years in transit and if they ever dreamed of visiting their homeland again.

I thought, too, of the Norse concept of *hamingja*, which is sometimes translated as luck or fortune. The Norse believed that a person's *hamingja* was a female entity that carried the soul of the family. According to Daniel McCoy, the spirit was typically passed down through family lines. "Naming a newborn child after a relative would ensure, or at least increase the likelihood, that the relative's *hamingja* would be passed down to the child," he writes in *The Viking Spirit: An Introduction to Norse Mythology and Religion.* "Sometimes it seems like the dying or dead person could decide to whom his or her *hamingja* went, and at other times it seems like the *hamingja* decided herself. A living person could also lend his or her *hamingja* to others to accompany them on particular endeavors in which extra luck would be of great use, such as a battle or a long and perilous journey."

I loved the idea that my family might have its own spirit, passed down from generation to generation, born in the wilds of the North but still present, perhaps, on this country road in the middle of the Midwest. Maybe the kinship I sensed with Gudrid, in particular, was because she was a *hamingja* for me. *Viga-Glum's Saga* has a *hamingja* so tall that her shoulders touched two separate mountains. I looked around me, trying to spot anything out of the ordinary. If Gudrid or another *hamingja* was there, she was well hidden.

Shaking off my musings, I drove several miles more to reach my next destination: Glenwood Lutheran Church, the parish that was home to four generations of my family. Built of limestone and topped by a tall spire, it was an impressive sight as I came over the last hill, looking little different from the years when I attended church services and Sunday school classes there.

Glenwood was one of the earliest Norwegian Lutheran parishes in the region, with roots that go back to 1854. For decades its services were conducted in Norwegian, but as time passed, the connection to the old ways lessened, at Glenwood and at other Norwegian-language churches. According to the historian Odd Lovoll, this led to problems when the first-generation immigrants were approaching death: they wanted to be buried "in Norwegian" even though American-born pastors usually weren't fluent in the language. One pastor did his best to accommodate the wishes of the family but mixed up the word *flesh* with the similarly sounding Norwegian word *flesk*, which means pork. As a result, during the service he comforted the mourners by assuring them that their deceased loved one would be resurrected in the pork. I would guess they were probably too polite to correct him to his face, though they tsk-tsked about it later.

I parked my car and sat looking at the church for some time. My ancestors had probably helped build it from stone quarried just down the road, though I couldn't know for certain whether the church was simply a social outlet for them or if they were believers in its doctrines. Many immigrants, after all, were happy to escape the strictures of the Norwegian state church and never attended services again in their new home. But for those who remained Lutheran, like most of my relatives, the church was one of the pillars of their community, a tie to home as well as to their fellow Norwegians.

And then, one more stop: the small cemetery just down the road from the church, a quiet enclave ringed by trees and surrounded by fields. I got out of the car and wandered amid its rows, feeling quite at home. I'd been there many times growing up, though the lack of interest in my family about previous generations meant that I knew where my grandparents were buried, but no one else. This time, I spotted many familiar names from my family tree, from great uncles and aunts to more distant relatives. It had taken me a long time to get to this silent reunion of my deceased relatives, but I was finally here.

On the edge of our family plot, I found the stone for Hans and Sila. Their marker was handsome, made of carved limestone and standing about five feet tall, with words chiseled in Norwegian. I recognized *født* for birth and *død* for death, but the script at the bottom was indecipherable, worn enough that I couldn't have read it even if I knew the language. They are buried together, with Hans's name on the north side of the marker and Sila's on the south. In the end, these landless peasants had done pretty well for themselves. I didn't want to brag about them, realizing how profoundly non-Scandinavian that was, but still, I was proud of them.

I remembered standing at Leif Eriksson's house at L'Anse aux Meadows, that treeless, windy spot on the edge of North America. Perhaps I was getting too fanciful after all my musings during the weekend, but it seemed as if I'd knit the two places together and, in the process, parts of me as well. Because of these long-dead people and these far-flung places, I am who I am. They don't totally explain me, but standing there, I felt like I'd been given another piece of my own puzzle.

Before I left that peaceful spot, I told Hans and Sila how happy I was that they finally ended up with their own piece of land in perpetuity.

Built around 1180, the Borgund Church is the best-preserved stave church in Norway. (PHOTO BY BOB SESSIONS)

10

A Visit to the Holy Land

-·✱·-

In August of 1903, a Norwegian farmer named Oskar Rom traveled sixty miles to visit the University Museum of Antiquities in Kristiana (now Oslo). When he asked to see its director, he was at first given the brush-off. The museum was in the process of moving, he was told, and the director didn't have time to see him. Oskar persisted, saying he wanted to report that he'd found a Viking ship buried on his property near the Oslo Fjord, a recently purchased plot of land known as the Oseberg farm. "Let me show you something," he said, pulling out an intricately carved piece of wood inlaid with silver.

When the director saw it, he decided he wasn't too busy to talk to Oskar after all—and within twenty-four hours, he'd cleared his schedule so he could investigate the site in person. This was no Kensington Rune Stone. Oskar did indeed have a Viking burial on his land, the most complete ever found, a site that gives us an intriguing, and puzzling, window into the Norse world.

Archaeologists spent more than twenty years restoring what they excavated from Oskar's farm, piecing together both the boat and the story of its origin. In the year 834, the vessel was hauled onto land and filled with the goods that two high-status Vikings would need for eternity. Their bodies were laid out on a bed on its deck and surrounded by luxury goods that included an ornately carved wagon, embroidered tapestries, imported silk textiles, and five carved animal heads, as well as more utilitarian items such as kitchen utensils, looms, sleds, beds, tents, oil lamps, and storage chests. Fifteen horses, six dogs, and two cows were sacrificed to accompany them. The entire lot was then covered with rocks and soil, creating a mound that grass eventually covered so that it blended into the farmland around it. Though it had been plundered at some point after the burial, the robbers left most of the artifacts behind, likely taking only the jewelry and other metal pieces that had once been interred with the bodies.

Of all the remarkable things about this archaeological site, this is perhaps the most surprising: the two people buried with the boat weren't Viking warriors or kings, but instead two women.

I knew quite a bit about the Oseberg boat before arriving at the Viking Ship Museum in Oslo, but when I saw it in person its sheer beauty overwhelmed me, just as it does anyone with a fascination for the Viking Age. You can read dozens of books about the beauty of Norse ships—their elegant lines and sinuous curves, their intricately carved ornamental flourishes and fierce animal heads atop their bows—but until you stand next to one in person, it's impossible to fully comprehend how awe-inspiring they are. And this is the most magnificent boat of them all, the very Platonic ideal of a Viking boat, a ship that can make taciturn maritime engineers gush in admiration and history nerds quiver in excitement.

First, I walked slowly around it, taking it in from different angles. The stout workhorse of a vessel I'd seen in Newfoundland, the *knarr* similar to the ones that brought Leif and his kin to Vinland, can't compare to this sleek thoroughbred of a boat. I stood at last directly beneath its bow, gazing upwards at the animal head that reared above me, a figure that resembled a serpent more than a dragon. At the other end of the vessel, I could see a tail that coiled upwards, making the entire ship look like the body of an immense animal. This was the opposite of Gudrid's unassuming spindle whorl at L'Anse Aux Meadows—this was a boat that shouted VIKING.

It was inevitable, of course, that I would go to Norway. To anyone who grew up in Decorah, Norway was the promised land, the place you dreamed of visiting from the time you were young. To make it a true genealogical pilgrimage, I took the family along: my two adult sons, Owen and Carl; my sister, Julie; and my husband, Bob, who'd fortuitously discovered from an ancestry test that he has some Scandinavian DNA (while it's not a competition, let me point out he has only a measly 5 percent).

By now the entire family had caught some of my Viking fever. I gave them a list of books to read on topics ranging from Norse mythology and history to contemporary Scandinavia, and I e-mailed them links to anything Viking-related (e.g., "Here's a really interesting piece on Norse iron smithing!"). As for me, I spent much of the winter poring over maps and guidebooks, planning a two-week trip that would begin in Oslo, head west to Bergen, and then go north to the city of Trondheim, which was the capital of Norway during the Viking Age.

After a flight that landed us in Oslo, we wandered its streets, slightly dazed from jet lag but fascinated by what we saw. The city reminded me of Minneapolis, though Oslo has a higher percentage of blonds. Many of its residents seemed preternaturally attractive and fit as they strode purposefully down its sidewalks, even more hearty and resolute than their Minnesota cousins. We toured sites that included Vigeland Park, a green-lawned enclave that's home to more than two hundred sculptures by artist Gustav Vigeland, and the Fram Museum, which tells the story of the Norwegian polar expeditions of the late-nineteenth and early-twentieth centuries. The bravery and fortitude of the explorers as they endured brutal cold and extreme deprivation reinforced my growing sense that the Norwegians belong to a subspecies of *Homo sapiens* with extraordinary resilience.

As we explored the city, I continued to puzzle over what I'd learned at the Viking Ship Museum on our first afternoon. My thoughts kept returning to the Oseberg ship, one of three Viking Age boats on display there. Constructed from oak about a dozen years before it was buried, by Norse standards it wasn't particularly large, having space for just fifteen pairs of rowers. It was likely used to cruise along the shore rather than sail across open water. With its graceful lines and decorative designs on bow and stern, the boat was clearly built to impress—the symbolic equivalent, perhaps, of a wealthy person's yacht.

The grave goods found with the ship are equally significant. The elaborately carved cart is the most impressive of these artifacts, a four-wheeled vehicle that on its front bears an image of a man in a pit of snakes while its back panel is decorated with cats. The five animal heads—which might be dogs, bears, or mythological creatures—also exhibit exceptional craftsmanship. About twenty inches in length, they might have been affixed to posts as decorations or used in rituals. One of the quirkiest pieces is a bucket that bears two identical enamel figures at the base of the handle: each is of a man with a serene expression seated in a lotus position. It has been dubbed the Buddha bucket, though the design is unlikely to be of Asian origin.

Who were the women who went off to eternity so well-equipped? One was between seventy and eighty years of age, a woman who likely died of cancer; the other was around fifty. For years scholars thought that the elder woman might be Queen Åsa, the grandmother of King Harald Fairhair, though that theory has fallen out of favor. Maybe the younger woman was the servant and the elder her mistress, or the other way around. We do know that both ate a diet rich in meat, unlike less well-to-do Vikings who consumed mostly fish.

The most fascinating theory of all, at least to me, is that one of these women was a religious leader of some sort. It's known that carts were used in Norse religious processions, and those cats on the back panel might reference Freya's chariot being pulled by cats. Some have further speculated that the elder woman was a *völva*, a female spiritual leader and healer, in part because the grave goods included several artifacts that could have been used in rituals, including a staff or wand, a metal rattle, and the five carved animal heads. The elder woman also had a pouch on her belt containing cannabis seeds, though it's not known whether they were for the planting of hemp that could be made into rope or textiles, for pain relief, or for religious use.

I thought of Kari Tauring and her Völva Stav Guild in Minneapolis, and then of Thorbjorg, the seeress who'd worked her magic with Gudrid's help on that cold winter night in Greenland so long ago. If Thorbjorg had lived in Norway instead of back-of-beyond Greenland, I bet she would have traveled to eternity in a richly appointed boat like the Oseberg ship.

SEARCHING FOR ANCESTORS

After a weekend in Oslo, we boarded a train for a seven-hour journey to the western coastal city of Bergen. As we left the city, picturesque scenes of lush pastures and tidy farms flew by outside the window, giving way to increasingly rugged landscapes as we climbed higher in the mountains: forested valleys, waterfalls, crystalline rivers, glaciers, rugged cliffs, and alpine meadows. I could see why this route is lauded as one of the most beautiful train journeys in the world.

Fighting sleepiness after lunch, I listened to the soft voices of a group of elderly women sitting behind me. Their conversation stirred long-forgotten memories of hearing my three great-aunts, who'd lived together their entire lives, speaking Norwegian among themselves when I visited them as a child. I closed my eyes, lulled by the singsong of the women's voices and the slight swaying of the train, which felt like it was taking me back in time as well as across the Norwegian landscape.

Finally arriving in Bergen, we were met at the train station by strangers who invited us into their home for three days. Well, technically they weren't strangers, at least to me. Inta

Tove and I had been classmates in elementary school during the years when her father taught Norwegian at Luther College. We'd lost touch after her parents made the decision to return with their family to Norway, but when a mutual friend heard I was going to Bergen, she suggested I contact her. I was hesitant at first, thinking that maybe I should connect instead with some of the distant cousins I had in Norway. But it felt awkward to thrust myself upon total strangers, remembering again the week that the Griswolds in *National Lampoon's European Vacation* spent with the puzzled Germans.

So I wrote to Inta Tove. "Maybe we could have dinner together when we're in Bergen," I suggested in an e-mail. To my surprise, she responded with an invitation to stay for several days with her and her family. "All five of us?" I replied. "Of course," she wrote.

At the train station I recognized her immediately, because even after forty-six years her smile was the same. We hugged, and she introduced us to her husband, Helge, who greeted us warmly as well. Then we drove up the winding, narrow streets of Bergen to their house perched on the side of one of the seven mountains overlooking the city. Inta Tove told us we'd sleep in a downstairs apartment at her sister's but come to her house for meals. I mentally added another characteristic to my growing list of superhuman Norwegian traits: extraordinary hospitality.

That impression was reinforced during our stay with Inta Tove and her extended family. After touring on our own during the day, we returned to her home in the late afternoons for evenings of socializing. Helge is a Lutheran pastor who works in the administration of the national church, while Inta Tove teaches occupational therapy at a local university. Their two children, Simen and Kristin, lived with them, and Inta Tove's two sisters and their families have homes within a few blocks. This loving and accomplished clan seemed to live in a Nordic paradise, with their houses decorated with understated Scandinavian sophistication, their environmentally friendly electric cars, and their formidable athleticism, which left us panting as we walked with them on the steep hills of their neighborhood.

Not to mention their fondness for candles, which they used for every social event, including breakfast.

One evening Inta Tove and Helge hosted an outdoor dinner party for us with their neighbors and friends, complete with hand-knitted wool sweaters draped over the chairs in case anyone got cold. As we ate, I brought up my quest to explore my Scandinavian origins.

"Have any of you had your DNA tested?" I asked them, adding that many of our American friends had done so.

"It's not very common here at all," one answered. "Why should we? We know who we are. We're Norwegian."

Which made sense, of course. In the United States, almost everyone is a mix of ethnicities, the product of centuries of immigration from many parts of the world, but the story is different in Norway, which historically has had much lower rates of immigration. If your parents or grandparents started over from scratch in a new locale, as is true for countless Americans, your roots don't go nearly as deep as those of people in Norway. Many families there have lived in the same communities— sometimes even in the same house—for centuries.

My questions on their knowledge of the Vikings delineated another cultural divide. "We learned about them in school, but you have to remember that there's a lot of Norwegian history to cover, and the Viking Age is only a small part of it," said a neighbor. "And they were pretty violent, weren't they? I think you Americans are more interested in them than we are."

Later that evening, Inta Tove told me more about her own story of immigration. She'd been born in the United States when her father was teaching at Luther College. While her family had traveled back to Norway for visits, she was thoroughly American when her parents decided to move back to their homeland when she was eleven years old.

"It was a huge change for me and our family," she said. "I wasn't fluent in Norwegian, and I remember struggling to learn the language when we moved here. I'd practice the extra Norwegian vowels over and over, trying to get their pronunciation right. And I missed the small-town life we had in Decorah, which was so easy and comfortable." Hearing her stories, I thought of all the immigrants who'd come to America from Norway and were homesick for their homeland for the rest of their lives. Inta Tove's experience gave a new twist to that pattern of immigration, but the difficulties of being uprooted and having to start over in a new land remain similar, no matter what the particulars of geography or the time period.

On our last day in Bergen we toured the Bryggen, a historic wharf area that was once home to the Hanseatic League, a German trade network that operated in northern Europe from the fourteenth through the mid-sixteenth centuries. Its brightly painted, timbered buildings lining one side of Bergen's harbor provided a colorful backdrop for the tourists who thronged the district.

Wandering through the streets a few blocks away from the harbor, I was delighted to come upon a statue of my old friend Snorri Sturluson, the compiler of Norse stories in the *Prose Edda*. There he stood on a pedestal, looking dignified and wise, holding a book in his left hand. Remembering the descriptions I'd read of his hefty weight and scandalous life, I gazed upwards with considerable amusement: Snorri has undergone a makeover.

I strolled back to the harbor area in a contemplative mood, watching as the rest of the family walked ahead of me. I saw how Carl, especially, blended seamlessly into the mix of people, his tall frame and blond hair making him look perfectly at home amid the largely Scandinavian crowd. If Hans and Sila and my other ancestors had decided to stay instead of emigrating, we would be among the people here speaking Norwegian. I would have made a fine citizen of Norway, I thought, given my love for candles, knitting, and the outdoors. And if I'd grown up here, I bet I'd even be less embarrassingly awkward on skis.

Goodness knows, I felt an undeniable sense of kinship with these people. I remembered a comment made by a friend who lives in Holland, Michigan, who'd had a similar sense of familiarity when she visited the region in the Netherlands from which many of the ancestors of the town's residents had emigrated. "It was weird," she said. "They looked like the people in my hometown, and they even *walked* the same."

Coming at last to the edge of the wharf, I savored the smell of salt in the air and the sight of the boats bobbing in the harbor before me. I realized that Hans and Sila had stood somewhere near here before they left on a boat for America. Because of them, I knew that I would remain an outsider here, no matter how great my fascination with this culture. I was destined to always look at Norway from the outside, no matter how blue my eyes.

IMPOSSIBLY BEAUTIFUL NORWAY

From Bergen, we headed north by rental car to the fjord region, where jagged-edged mountains border deep inlets from the sea. The road periodically plunged through tunnels or clung to narrow strips of land next to the water, which was spanned in some places by bridges and in others by ferries that took us from one shore to the next, putt-putting smoothly where longboats once sailed.

The seamlessly integrated transportation network is a testimony to the ingenuity of engineers as well as the great wealth enjoyed by Norway thanks to its petroleum industry. Vast reserves of oil were discovered in the North Sea in 1969, and unlike many other oil-rich nations that have been plagued by corruption and mismanagement, Norway has handled its fiscal windfall responsibly, using it to fund infrastructure, social services, and a wide array of public works. The fact that much of its financial stability is based on fossil fuels doesn't sit well with many environmentally conscious Norwegians, but few will deny that the discovery has brought huge benefits to the nation. Thanks to North Sea oil, what was once one of the poorest countries in Europe is now one of the richest nations in the world.

"If you want to be poor in Norway, you pretty much have to live up on a remote mountain with no postal service," a resident of Oslo told me. "Otherwise they'll hunt you down and force you to take checks from the government. On the other hand, it's hard to be rich in Norway, because the taxes are so high. But most people are content with being somewhere in the middle."

As we drove, I wondered what my ancestors would think of Norway today. Its wealth would likely be inconceivable to them, these peasants who forged a precarious living on rocky slivers of farmland. The ease of travel alone would amaze them. In their day, trips involved either arduous journeys up and over the mountains or circuitous water journeys, which meant that most people rarely traveled and got used to living without many neighbors around, no doubt contributing to the famous Scandinavian reticence. The generation of immigrants, the ones who decided that their prospects were so poor that they might as well leave, would likely have second thoughts today, especially when they heard about those checks thrust upon people by the government.

What hasn't changed over the centuries, however, is the landscape, which in the fjord region in particular is so stunning that I quickly run out of superlatives to describe it. It's as if God decided to double his bet on beauty when he was making this part of Norway, just for the fun of it. You like mountains? You like water? Let's put 'em together and see what happens! Each bend of the road presented us with another spectacular vista, the brilliant green vegetation and rocky crags of the mountains reflected in the shimmering blue waters of the fjords. Adding to the splendor was the ever-shifting weather, which wreathed the mountains in mist one moment and then sent shafts of sunlight piercing through the clouds the next. We eventually had to speak sternly to Bob, in fact, because he kept veering off so often to take pictures, once barely missing an oncoming car.

"I don't want to die in Norway, even if it is one of the most beautiful places in the world," Owen announced from the back seat.

After an overnight in a town overlooking the Sogne Fjord (the longest and deepest fjord in Norway), we set out for Lærdal, a municipality that sits at the eastern end of the waterway. This is the region where Hans and Sila had lived, and no doubt many of my other ancestors as well, given that people of their social class generally stayed put. Once we got away from the shore of the fjord the scenery calmed down a little, but it was still idyllic, with forest-covered mountains and prosperous-looking farms in the valleys, their red houses and barns often encircled by white picket fences. As we drove, I mentally contrasted the landscape before me to the gently rolling hills of Iowa. I felt bad for my home state until I realized that almost all countries have to concede defeat when compared with Norway's beauty.

Our destination was the Borgund Church where both Hans and Sila had been baptized, which by happy accident (thank you, Web of Wyrd!) just happens to be the best-preserved stave church in Norway. These medieval structures are the nation's most distinctive architectural form. Constructed of wood, their name comes from the vertical posts (*stav* in Norwegian) that anchor their walls. More than a thousand stave churches were built in Norway over a period of about two hundred years, beginning in the twelfth century and continuing until the Black Death swept through the countryside in 1349. Today only twenty-eight survive.

When the Vikings became Christian, it was natural for them to use wood instead of stone for the building of churches. They had so much of it, for one thing, and the country was full of master craftsmen with long experience in building ships and wooden structures. They copied the general form of the stone churches of Europe but added details from their native traditions. Church roofs, for example, bear similarities to the inside of a Viking ship, though one was used to sail into heaven, and the other to go raiding. Artisans incorporated pagan elements into some of these churches, including dragon heads like those on Viking ships and decorative carvings of intertwined animals, which were common in Norse designs. Like the Norwegian parents who continued to name their children variations of Thor long after the nation became Christian, bits and pieces of the pagan past lived on in these churches.

As we came over a hill from the parking lot and saw the Borgund Church for the first time, I blinked my eyes several times to make sure what I was seeing was really there. The Borgund Church is extravagantly, impossibly picturesque, even by Norwegian standards. Situated in a rural valley surrounded by mountains, it has five sets of steeply pitched, tiered roofs that culminate in a tower. Just beneath, four dragon heads extend far into the air, looking as if they're trying to leap away from the building. The exterior of the church has weathered so much through the centuries that it appears to be almost black, the somber color adding to its dramatic appearance. It looked, in short, exactly like the sort of church recently converted Vikings would build.

Before entering the building we toured the visitor center, a separate structure of stylish, modern design. There we learned that stave churches were built in other countries in northern Europe during the Middle Ages, but outside of Norway, only a handful have survived. Even in Norway, most of the remaining structures were either added to or rebuilt at some point, changing their original appearance. Because the Borgund Church has had very few alterations, it is a cultural and religious landmark of international stature. Built around 1180, it served as a place of worship until 1868, when another church was constructed nearby, a building in which services are still held.

A short walk brought us to the stave church itself, which is surrounded by a graveyard bordered by a low wall of rocks. The closer we got to the building, the more imposing it seemed, its multitiered roof looming high above us. Stepping inside, however, we discovered that the interior of the church was surprisingly small, especially given the huge amount of wood that went into its construction. Only the ground level was used for worship, while the rest of the building between floor and ceiling was open, a shadowy and mysterious space.

I'd expected to spend my time here ruminating on the story of Hans and Sila, but the heavy, overwhelming presence of the building, with its thick walls and massive beams and buttresses, crowded other thoughts out of my mind. This place felt immeasurably old, making me wonder if it had been built on the site of a pagan temple, as was commonly done in the early years of Christianity in Europe. It seemed to me as if this had been a holy place for a very long time, much longer than eight centuries.

Walking around the sanctuary, I tried to figure out why this place felt so different from other churches I'd been in. Part of the reason is that wood, even after it's been cut from a tree, is alive in a way that stone isn't. What's more, as I stood looking upward at the roof far above me, it felt almost as if I were *inside* a tree. Breathing in the scent of the ancient timbers, I wondered if the builders of this place had viewed the wood as sacred, despite their Christian faith. Maybe that's why they used so much lumber to create what is quite a modest-sized worship space. Those shrewd Vikings might have been hedging their metaphysical bets, building a worship space where their pagan ancestors wouldn't have felt entirely out of place. Perhaps they were trying to create a subtle echo of Yggdrasil, the world tree.

I remembered reading that on one side of the Borgund Church, scholars have deciphered runes that include a reference to the Norns, the supernatural beings who decide the fate of all humans: "The Norns did both good and evil, great toil they created for me." Like that long-ago worshiper, I also felt that this church seemed to have pagan sinews intertwined with its Christianity.

Then I shook my head and returned to reality, watching as the rest of my family wandered around the building. They, too, seemed to sense that this was a remarkable holy place, speaking in hushed voices as they looked upwards with expressions of awe on their faces. "This place is like a church, and yet not a church," Carl said to me. "Something about the dragons on top and the dark walls make me feel like we're protected in here."

At last I stepped outside, the sunlight brilliant after the dimness inside the building. It was time to connect my own story with the history of this place. I wandered amid the graves, looking for a person who might have known Hans and Sila. It didn't take long to find one: he rested under a worn headstone that bore the name of Ingeleiv Voldum, born in 1836. He would have been fourteen when my great-great-grandparents walked out of the valley for the last time. I wondered if he'd waved them goodbye.

HANS, AT LAST

One more place beckoned us, though I wasn't sure I'd be able to find its exact location: the farm where Hans lived before emigrating. Jerry Paulson at the Norwegian American Genealogical Center in Wisconsin had found references to several farms associated with his family, but a plot of land named Arvid Brøyn seemed to pop up most often. Because farm names are typically passed down from generation to generation in Norway, he thought there was a good chance I'd be able to locate it on my trip there.

At the church's visitor center, I'd asked directions from a staff member, a man who knew the general direction of the farm, but not its exact location. "It's just a few kilometers from here, I think," he said. "You can probably find someone to ask once you're in the general area."

The problem was that I quickly became lost once we left the main highway. Was this the bridge the man referred to, or was it the larger one down the road? Did he say two right turns and then a left one, or was it the other way around? I scoured my notes, trying to remember exactly what he'd said, hoping that I hadn't mixed up right and left like I often do.

"You'd think you'd be better at directions, given the fact you're descended from Leif Eriksson," Bob said as he waited for me to tell him which way to turn at an intersection.

"Turn left," I said, ignoring him, because with only a fraction of true Viking DNA, he couldn't fully understand the significance of my quest.

"You're sure?"

"Of course not. But keep driving."

We drove slowly down a narrow road that wound through a valley bisected by a small river, looking in vain for a place where we could ask directions. Then I spotted a sign that said "Björaker Camping." I remembered that Hans's name in Norway had been Hans Ørbech Henrikssøn Bjørager and that people in that era often used the name of the farm where they were living as their last name.

"Follow that sign!" I told Bob, feeling a little like Leif spotting the coast of Vinland through the fog.

A short distance down the road, we pulled into a farm that had a few small camping huts in its yard. A white-haired woman came out of the house, ready to check us in, but when I explained our reason for being there she didn't seem upset at losing customers. "You're not the first person who's come here looking for ancestors, though it's been a number of years since the last one," she said, in accented but excellent English. "This farm's been in my husband's family for generations. He's not here now but I'll do my best to help you. Wait here."

A couple of minutes later she returned, carrying a copy of the same local history book that Jerry Paulson had shown me in the genealogy library in Wisconsin. Spreading it open on the hood of our car, she flipped through its pages until she found the section dealing with land records in her area.

"Hans was a *husmann*, a sharecropper," I offered. "The census said he lived on a farm named Arvid Brøyn. Does that help?"

The woman nodded. "At that time, this was the main farm, but there were tenant farmers on several smaller plots of land around us," she answered. "Your relative's place isn't far from here at all."

So that's how we ended up on the tiny patch of land where Hans had lived before leaving for America. By Norwegian standards it wasn't particularly scenic, just a hillside with more rocks than soil, not far from the river. The more picturesque part of the neighborhood was at the other end of the valley, closer to the Borgund Church. The land didn't look like it was still farmed or even used as a pasture for animals.

"We made it!" I said, linking my arms through those of my sons, feeling like I'd just won a gold medal in the Olympics (I'd never win one for skiing, but maybe I could be a contender if they offered ones for genealogy). "Julie, come here. Let's take a picture."

My sister joined us, and we lined up so Bob could snap a photo. In one sense it was the most boring picture we took in Norway, much less scenic than all the ones in which we'd posed in front of mountains or fjords or eighteenth-century buildings. It shows the four of us in front of a hillside with some patches of tufty grass and a lot of rocks—but of all the photos from our trip, it means the most to me.

Then I knelt down, scraping away the rocks to find some dirt. I gathered a couple of handfuls of soil and put them carefully into a small plastic bag that I tucked into my pocket. Next I took something out of my other pocket: a stone from the farm where I'd grown up, just a few miles from the farm where Hans and Sila had lived. I looked at it in my hand, its inconsequential weight symbolizing all that had happened to Hans after he left his home here and all that had happened to me so that I could stand in this place.

Then I threw the rock up onto the hillside, as hard as I could, spinning a new thread in the Web of Wyrd, linking Iowa and Norway once again.

An image of St. Olaf stands above the entrance to Nidaros Cathedral in Trondheim, Norway. (PHOTO BY BOB SESSIONS)

11

Travels with St. Olaf

-:✶:-

During his lifetime in the eleventh century, he was known as Olaf the Fat or Olaf the Stout. After his death he became St. Olaf, and later he was given the even grander title of the Eternal King of Norway, making him a kind of Scandinavian King Arthur. But for the second week of my trip to Norway, he was simply Olaf, a man I was hoping to get to know better.

Bob and I began the week by dropping Owen and my sister at the Bergen airport. While they were returning to their ordinary lives, the two of us and Carl were headed north to the city of Trondheim, the Viking Age capital of Norway and the site of Nidaros Cathedral, the place where the bones of St. Olaf are said to rest. We took our time, spending several days traversing a landscape filled with even more spectacular fjords and mountains than we'd seen before (just when you think you've reached the zenith of beauty in Norway, the country pulls something else out of its hat). As we traveled, I realized that while visiting the farm where Hans once lived had been the culmination of my genealogy pilgrimage, my second week in Norway was more of a spiritual quest. In journeying to Trondheim, I hoped to gain a better understanding of the double helix of my religious DNA.

True to my Viking heritage, I've been as much of a wanderer in my spiritual life as I am in my professional one. After my Lutheran upbringing in Decorah I became a Wiccan, a pagan path that has a lot in common with the beliefs of my Norse ancestors, though without the blood sacrifices. Following that I was a Unitarian Universalist for several years, and then I returned to the Christian fold again as an Episcopalian, but with a generous dollop of Buddhism.

My genealogical research made me wonder what my ancestors would think about my religious eclecticism. I was pretty sure the generations closest to me would disapprove, given the sternness of nineteenth-century Lutheran theology, but I thought my Viking forebears would be less judgmental, given how readily many of them adopted the faith of whatever region in which they settled. (A sixth-century statue of the Buddha was even found in an archaeological dig in Helgo, Sweden—an indication, perhaps, that one of those Viking warriors was intrigued enough by a faith he encountered on his Eastern travels to bring back a religious artifact.) And while my ancestors had an unfortunate habit of raiding monasteries, it was only because that's where the gold and silver were, not because they held a grudge against Christianity or wanted to assert their own religious beliefs.

I was eager to visit Nidaros Cathedral in part because I knew that during the Middle Ages it was one of northern Europe's important pilgrimage destinations. I figured the church would be a good place to put my spiritual DNA under a microscope, here at this holy site where Norwegian kings were crowned and where the life of the most famous Scandinavian saint is honored.

I was curious, too, about how contemporary Norwegians viewed Christianity. Though Inta Tove and Helge and their friends had been positive in their comments on religion, I recalled an interchange I had with the Norwegian national tourism office when I was planning our trip. In response to my question about Viking sites, the public relations representative gave a long list of suggestions for where I might travel for research on my book. When I asked about religious landmarks, however, I was given a polite brush-off: "I really do not have any suggestions for spiritual heritage sites," wrote the official.

I knew that Norway is one of the most secular nations in the world, but still—he was a government-employed professional, someone whose job it is to know the cultural riches of his nation. To hear him so blithely dismiss its religious traditions made me want to protest to him about the beauty of the stave churches in Norway and the fact that for millennia its people believed that the forests, springs, and mountains around them sheltered supernatural forces. For most of Norway's history, the numinous intersected with the ordinary in countless places.

I was journeying to Nidaros, I realized, to examine both my own faith and that of Norway.

A SAINT WITH A BROADSWORD

The category of "Viking Saints" isn't overcrowded, but amid that small group, St. Olaf (also known as Olav) stands tall. The usual pious adjectives of meek, holy, and gentle don't get used much in relation to this influential figure. Born in 995, Olaf Haraldsson was descended from Harald Fairhair, the first king of Norway. He went on his first raid at the tender age of twelve and for the rest of his life went to battle an average of twice a year, according to one admiring biographer.

One of Olaf's earliest expeditions was to England, where he participated in a raid that resulted in the death of the Archbishop of Canterbury, who later became St. Alphege. Olaf was said to have delivered the fatal blow, thus making him one of the few (if any) saints to have killed another saint. Later he raided in Brittany, France, and Spain before returning to his homeland in 1015, where he proclaimed himself king and made the city of Nidaros, which later became Trondheim, his capital.

At some point during his raiding years, Olaf became a Christian, though knowing exactly what that conversion meant

to him is difficult. Scandinavia had lagged behind the rest of
Europe in adopting Christianity, but by this time the faith was
making greater inroads in the northern lands. Political leaders often converted for practical purposes, wanting to forge
alliances and promote trade with the rest of Europe. Christianity was also attractive because it increased national unity
through centralized church structures and gave the stamp of
divine authority to Scandinavian kings (paganism had always
been pretty loosey-goosey on these matters, with no dogma
or institutional hierarchy). The elaborate rituals of Christianity impressed the Norse, too. Many guessed that the new god
must be superior to theirs, given how wealthy and powerful the
Christian nations were.

Two decades before, a previous king of Norway, Olaf
Trygvesson, had tried to convert the nation to the new faith,
but his favorite evangelism methods of trickery, torture, murder, and bribery had left a good share of the populace only
nominally Christian. The new King Olaf was determined to
make Norway a genuinely Christian nation. He was somewhat
less brutal in his efforts, but like the other Olaf relied on violence when faced with reluctant converts. He was also unpopu-
lar because he punished people for piracy and looting, which
were, of course, the modus operandi of many Vikings. Resistance to Olaf's rule grew among the chieftains, and in 1028 he
was forced to flee to Russia.

Two years later, Olaf came back to Norway, but his trium-
phal return didn't go as he hoped. In 1030 he was killed at
the Battle of Stiklestad, sixty miles northeast of Trondheim.
In death, however, Olaf got some lucky breaks that made up
for his unfortunate end. Soon after his death there was a solar
eclipse, which people took as a sign from God of his sanctity.
His body was hidden in a sandbank for safekeeping, and a year
later when it was exhumed, eyewitnesses reported that it hadn't
decayed. Even better, miraculous healings began to occur in its
presence. Recognizing a golden opportunity when he saw one,
a local bishop declared Olaf a saint and put his relics into the
bishop's own church of St. Clement. After the cult of St. Olaf

grew in popularity, his shrine was moved to another site, one that would eventually become Nidaros Cathedral.

Thus rough-hewn Olaf, he of the portly figure and swinging broadsword, was transformed after his death into a reverent and noble leader, the very model of a Christian king. His fame spread beyond the borders of Scandinavia, with churches built in his honor throughout northern Europe (including in York, England, where the Jorvik Vikings lived). Olaf was honored as far away as Constantinople, where he became the last Western saint recognized by the Eastern Orthodox Church before the Great Schism of 1054.

But Olaf's greatest posthumous achievement was this: more than anyone else, he's given credit for transforming Norway into a Christian nation, despite being oh-so-Viking in his temperament.

Thanks in part to the many pilgrims who visited the shrine of St. Olaf, the city of Nidaros prospered, remaining the nation's capital until 1217 (the name of Trondheim was adopted three centuries later). The church erected over Olaf's bones started as a simple wooden structure but eventually became the impressive building of today, a massive structure of gray soapstone that stands in the city center. Blending Romanesque and Gothic styles, the cathedral's beauty is tinged with sternness, a reflection of the sternness of Norwegian Christianity—or so it seemed to me as I stood before it, having arrived at last in the city of Trondheim, the final stop of my Norway journey. Gazing upwards at its facade of carved statues, I imagined they were looking down on me with a faint air of disapproval, perhaps sensing my coat-of-many-colors religious identity.

It didn't help that the sunny weather we'd enjoyed for most of our time in Norway had turned gray and rainy, the dark sky serving as a somber backdrop for the cathedral. I thought of the Borgund Church, another impressive spiritual sanctuary but one that still has some Norse paganism in its bones. Nidaros Cathedral, in contrast, is unmistakably, thoroughly Christian.

Inside the church, I joined a tour led by a young woman who, like most Norwegians, spoke fluent English. She

recounted the story of St. Olaf with diplomatic honesty, admit-
ting the contradictions between his life and his reputation for
sanctity. His remains, she told us, are said to rest beneath the
high altar of the church, though this hasn't been conclusively
proven. She then recounted the history of the building, which
was begun in 1070 and constructed over three centuries. After
the Reformation separated the Protestant and Roman Catholic branches of Christianity, the cathedral became the seat of
Lutheran bishops. Periodically damaged by fires, it was in sore
need of repair when major renovations were begun in the late-
nineteenth century.

After the tour I wandered the building, thinking of other
cathedrals I've visited around the world. Nidaros is among the
most beautifully restored I've seen, a reflection of its importance as a national symbol and the wealth of Norwegian society.
Despite my fondness for grand church architecture, however,
there was something about the building that left me cold. Just
a few people were wandering around inside, for one thing, and
it was largely devoid of the rich iconography that I love about
Catholic cathedrals. It seemed more of a civic monument than
a living holy place, though perhaps that was only because I
was visiting on a rainy afternoon when a northern chill nipped
around the edges of the building.

I felt restless and unsettled, regretting that our trip was near-
ing its end and pondering what I'd learned in the country of
my ancestors. I'd followed a circuitous route through the Web
of Wyrd to get to this spot. Thanks to my explorations I now
had a deepened understanding of the complexities of Norse
history and the culture and faith of my Lutheran ancestors, but
there was no denying that I felt little kinship with Nidaros, as
beautiful and impressive as it is. Much of what made Norse
history so fascinating to me—the larger-than-life passions, the
love of adventure and risk taking—seemed to be missing here,
and inside the church's walls I'd listened in vain for some inner
voice that gave me an answer to my own spiritual questions.

With a sigh, I headed out the front door of the church, leaving it behind without a backward glance.

ON THE CUSP BETWEEN RELIGIONS

While the Vikings were skilled at adapting to whatever they encountered, the same is true of Christianity, especially in the first years after it arrives in a new region. In Scandinavia, the lines between the old and new faiths remained fluid for several centuries after Olaf's death. As Christianity began to take root, many pagans considered Jesus just another deity and were happy to add him to their pantheon of gods. An Icelandic poem from this period, for example, depicts Christ sitting beside the Norns, the three goddesses of fate. During the transition between religions some people were buried with grave goods that included both Christian crosses and Thor's hammers. Most converts focused not on the suffering Jesus on the cross but on the triumphant Christ of the Last Judgment, who in early Christian images from Scandinavia often looks more than a little like Thor.

Because people were believed to be more trustworthy if they were Christian, many of the pragmatic Norse thought that if being sprinkled with water would get them better business deals, well, bring on the water. An added bonus was that free white shirts were often given at baptism, which meant that some Vikings underwent multiple baptisms to improve their wardrobes.

While practicality certainly played a role in the Norse conversion to Christianity, there was genuine religious conviction as well. Women in particular seem to have been leaders in the shift to Christianity. While many higher status Norse women enjoyed considerable autonomy, this wasn't true for those from the lower classes—and no woman of any class could hope to spend eternity in Valhalla, the paradise for warriors. Christianity, in contrast, taught that each woman had a soul and a place in heaven. The new religion also forbade the killing of unwanted infants, a practice that had always resulted in the deaths of more female babies than male ones.

One of the biggest changes brought by Christianity related to language and literacy. The clergy introduced the Latin alphabet and books made from vellum (the skin of calves) with writing done in ink. Norse runes had never been widely used among the populace, and when they were written down they were typically incised on stone or wood. The new-fangled books were a considerable upgrade in terms of ease of use, though for a long time writing was seen as inferior to the oral tradition.

The Norse belief in Ragnarök, the apocalypse in which almost all the gods would die and a new world would emerge, probably contributed to the ease of the transition as well. The Norse gods, after all, had foreseen their own demise. Their end came with the coming of Christianity, not with the prophesied battles and cataclysms, but the final result was the same.

One of the best indications of the transition was that fewer and fewer people were buried with grave goods. Pagans needed a lot of stuff to take with them into the afterlife; Christians didn't. And around 1110, the pagan rites at the great temple at Uppsala, Sweden, ended. While local ceremonies and customs no doubt continued for some time, Christianity became the dominant faith in Scandinavia.

Several centuries later, the Protestant Reformation brought more changes to the religious landscape of Norway. Scandinavia embraced Lutheranism with vigor, becoming even more Lutheran than Germany, which was the birthplace of the Reformation thanks to native son Martin Luther. King Christian III of Denmark-Norway (at that point the two countries were united) converted to Lutheranism and in 1537 made the Evangelical Lutheran faith the official religion. Monasteries and convents were dissolved, and by 1600, Lutheranism was firmly established—and that's why I grew up Lutheran in rural Iowa, all those years later.

It's a mystery to me why Norwegians embraced Lutheranism so wholeheartedly. Maybe these people who'd once been so violent knew they needed a tight lid to keep their Norse passions under control. Perhaps they regretted the cycle of bloodshed and revenge that had fueled much of their history and adopted a particularly buttoned-down version of Christianity to pay penance (imagine ISIS members in the Middle East deciding to become Quakers). Maybe it was a historical accident or something in the Scandinavian character. Most likely, it was a mix of many factors.

Whatever the reasons, as the centuries passed, the Norwegians settled into a particularly devout Lutheranism, with starched collars, strict rules, and a great emphasis on the dignity and power of the clergy. When I remember the sacrificial victims swinging from the trees in the sacred grove at Uppsala, I have to admit there were good reasons why the Norse left paganism behind, but still, there's a twinge of regret in me for the color, drama, and passion of that earlier era.

I remembered a passage I'd read by Tom Shippey in *Laughing Shall I Die: Lives and Deaths of the Great Vikings.* He says that for the Norse, the most admired characteristic of a warrior was his ability to laugh in the face of death. I thought of his words on that gray afternoon as I left Nidaros Cathedral, heading back outside into the rain, thinking not of the Christian God, but of the gods who'd gone before.

"A hero is defined not by victory but by defeat," writes Shippey. "Only in defeat can you show what you're really made of. Only in final defeat can you show that you will never give in. That's why the gods have to die as well. If they did not die, how could they show true courage? If they were really immortal and invulnerable, who would respect them?"

At our dinner party at Inta Tove and Helge's house, I'd asked the other guests about religious belief in Norway. Most of them attend church frequently, they replied, and the royal family, which is held in high esteem, are churchgoers. Norway's flag also bears a cross—all indications that Norway's Christian traditions are important. While many of the outward signs of religious life have been de-emphasized, the dinner guests said, the Christian values of caring for your neighbor and the poor are the wellspring of the generous social welfare net in Scandinavia. Even if their fellow citizens don't attend services regularly, they added, most of them still identify with Christianity and have their children baptized.

But they also admitted that religious affiliation is on the decline in all of Scandinavia. "For many people in Norway, I think exercise is their true religion," said one man ruefully. "That's what they organize their lives around."

Thinking of all the fit people I'd seen in Oslo and Bergen, it didn't seem like a terribly bad alternative for religious faith. I wondered, however, why these people who'd once been fierce pagans, and then fiercely committed Lutherans, had shed so much of their religious identity. Maybe the famed Norwegian connection to the outdoors, that urge to climb mountains, hike across country, and slalom down ski slopes, is due in part to hearing the spirits of the land calling them at some unconscious level. Perhaps they remember, deep within, what it means to view nature as filled with spirit and realize that what they find in churches can't compare to their experiences in their extravagantly beautiful outdoors.

The secular world would argue, of course, that Scandinavia hasn't lost very much and has simply jettisoned superstition. In some ways what's happened in Norway is simply the way of religions, all of which have an ebb and flow. Sometimes one faith is in ascendancy; sometimes another. Just as the Viking pagans probably thought the old ways would last forever (at least until Ragnarök), the Lutherans of the eighteenth and nineteenth centuries thought that their traditions were eternal. And what would both these groups make of modern Scandinavia, which has become one of the most secular nations in the world? Today about 70 percent of Norwegians consider themselves part of the Church of Norway, the state religion, but the country has one of the lowest rates of church attendance in the world, with only about two percent regularly attending services.

I'm not ready to make any predictions about the future of religion in Scandinavia; I know enough about the history of world religions to realize that just when you think you have the spirit figured out, it shape-shifts into something else. But I suspect that the Norwegians are more tied to their past than is immediately obvious, and the twin roots of paganism and Christianity still nourish their culture in unseen ways. Perhaps the reason that secularism is ascendant in modern Norway is simply that they're so materially comfortable—those checks arriving from the government without fail, fueled in part by the flow of wealth from North Sea oil. Impoverished Norway is a distant memory now, but if conditions change, perhaps some will seek comfort in the older traditions. Whether they will return to their pagan roots, to the Lutheranism of the more recent past, or to new faiths, I can't predict, but I suspect their bond to the land will continue, no matter what path they follow.

As for me, my time in Norway made me feel even closer to Gudrid the Far Traveler, my adopted foremother. By now I'd learned a great deal about her life, from what it was like to wear Viking clothing and what kind of house she lived in to her problematic sister-in-law. I was beginning to think I could guess a little more about her inner life, too, as I reflected more deeply about what it means to live on the cusp between two worldviews and two faiths. Gudrid alternated between the Old World and the New, between paganism and Christianity, between the world of rationality and the world of magic. One moment she was a devout Christian, and the next she was chanting the summoning songs for spirits. Like Gudrid, I also exist in a time of fluidity, when the familiar markers of my culture are changing. In the world of my childhood, Christianity was part of the air I breathed, but today the church—especially mainline Christianity—is shedding members at an accelerating rate, the opposite of what Gudrid experienced. She lived when the church was waxing; I live during its waning, at least in North America and Western Europe.

But I've always been intrigued by betwixt and between landscapes—the ones between life and death, between cultures, and between religions. That's where the most interesting things seem to happen, where the pot gets stirred and new developments arise. One thing I most admire about Gudrid, I realize, is the way she bridged those divisions with such grace.

While our fellow Vikings set out in search of treasure, Gudrid and I were on the hunt for riches of a different sort—experiences and adventure. She could have been content to stay on the Icelandic farm of her childhood, just as I could have in Iowa, but our restless spirits sent us on both inner and outer journeys. You might call us Vikings of the Spirit, each holding tight to our own shining thread as we make our way through the Web of Wyrd.

OUR LADY OF TRONDHEIM

After visiting the cathedral, Bob, Carl, and I wandered the streets of Trondheim, rubbing elbows with a mix of tourists, locals, and university students. Despite the light rain, the atmosphere was festive. We walked past restaurants with signs proclaiming a commitment to local, organic food and outdoor cafés where people sat talking animatedly to one another, then passed through an area where workers were setting up a sound system for a music festival to be held that weekend.

At last we came to our final destination in Trondheim: the Church of Our Lady, a stone church dating back to the twelfth century. As a fan of the Virgin Mary, I wanted to pay my respects to her there, especially because I knew she doesn't get a lot of attention in this nation where so many are secular and where most of those who are religious are Lutheran, a faith that doesn't have much devotion for Mary.

While the Church of Our Lady's operations are overseen by Nidaros Cathedral, the vibe inside the building felt different from that of the cathedral down the street—baroque rather than austere, intimate rather than monumental. A sign in its entryway listed some of the activities and services that go on within its walls, many geared to the city's less fortunate citizens. Even in Norway there are homeless and desperate people, and this church has a mission to help them.

In contrast to the impeccably restored Nidaros, the interior of the church was a bit shabby, but it was also full of life. A choir was practicing, their voices blending in a lively song accompanied by a drum. A circle of lighted candles on the floor in front of them lent a flickering light to the dimness of the sanctuary. Near the entrance was a coffee shop where a dozen ragtag customers were sitting, chatting with one another as they sipped their drinks.

After listening to the choir practice for a few minutes, I bought a cup of coffee and struck up a conversation with the clerk behind the counter. She told me she was a volunteer, like all the people working there, and explained that while the coffee shop is a gathering place for everyone, it especially welcomes those who don't have a community of their own. Payment for the food and drink is by donation, and no one is turned away if they can't pay.

"I'm not a Christian," she said. "I don't have any faith, really. But this is my church."

I pondered her words as we left the building, realizing they could be taken in two ways. I could be sad about the decline of religious faith in Norway, this land that birthed the wild Vikings and then the stalwart Lutherans, but I also admired the tenaciousness of the Norwegian spirit, which survives in those who hike and ski and resonate to the beauties of the Norwegian landscape. In Trondheim, this ancient site of pilgrimage, I could sense that spirit in the majesty of Nidaros, but even more in this scrappy little church where homeless people sit drinking coffee.

As evening fell, I wandered the city streets, trying to imprint every last detail of Norway in my mind before we flew out from the Trondheim airport in the morning. I thought about what this journey to the homeland of my ancestors had taught me about my *öorlog*, my own personal corner of the Web of Wyrd. I could see some of the threads much more clearly now. There's a green one that represents my ancestors who lived and died along the fjords, and one of blue for the generation that set out across the ocean to come to America. A glint of silver comes from the thread linking me to my Viking relations, the ones who were so fond of bringing back altarpieces when they raided Irish monasteries. The thread that ties me to Leif and Gudrid is bright gold, a reflection of how much they've inspired me. And all of them link back to Iowa, that fertile land that holds my roots no matter how far I travel.

The more I thought about it, the more unlikely and wondrous it all seemed, with its blend of violence and decorum, mayhem and piety, mountains and prairies, runes and gospels. It's a bit of a crazy quilt, this afghan knitted by the Norns at my birth, but it's me.

The Draken Harald Hårfagre, the largest Viking ship built in the modern era, has a dragon head on its prow. (PHOTO BY LORI ERICKSON)

Epilogue
On Board the Dragon

It was 100 degrees on board the Viking longboat, and in their skimpy shorts and T-shirts its crewmembers didn't look very Norse. "It's not a very Scandinavian sort of day," I said to a deckhand who was sweating heavily as he shifted a wooden crate from one part of the deck to another.

"Well, the Vikings did sail into the Mediterranean," he said. "But this would have been hot, even for them."

After several years of research I thought I was nearly done with my dive into Norse history and my ancestral roots, but when I heard that a Viking longboat was on the East Coast of the United States, I knew there was one more trip I needed to make. The *Draken Harald Hårfagre*, the largest Viking ship built in the modern era, was stopping at ports of call on the Eastern Seaboard, giving people the opportunity to come on board to learn about the Viking Age. Though I'd already seen several Viking boats, including the Oseberg ship in Oslo and replicas in L'Anse aux Meadows and Minnesota, they were museum pieces, the equivalent of seeing a tiger in a cage. The prospect of standing on the deck of an honest-to-goodness, seaworthy longboat was irresistible.

I was also curious why ordinary Americans, not just ones who'd caught a serious case of Viking fever, were coming to tour the boat. By now I'd found answers to many of my questions about my own genealogy, but I didn't fully understand why the larger world is so curious about the Vikings. Few ancient cultures provide much inspiration for the modern world, after all—nobody is very interested in the Sumerians or Assyrians, for example. But the Vikings, those disreputable bad boys of the Far North, continue to fascinate us. Perhaps I could find some answers in the unlikely Norse destination of Philadelphia.

What I hadn't anticipated was the heat and humidity, which made me wilt as soon as I stepped out of my hotel. Walking to the waterfront at a languid pace, I wondered what real Vikings would have done in such heat. I couldn't think of more inappropriate weather to tour a Norse ship.

My first sight of the *Draken*, however, made me momentarily forget my discomfort. From a distance the vessel docked in the city's harbor looked almost like a child's toy, a lone wooden boat amid fiberglass pleasure craft. As I drew closer, its graceful lines came into better focus, and I could see familiar elements, including its arched dragon's head and tall mast. My pace quickened, and a few minutes later I was at last standing on board a Viking longboat, taking in all the details of this living incarnation of the vessels that had carried my ancestors: the wide, broad deck with mast towering overhead, the smell of tar, the gentle rocking of the water. I grinned as I gazed upwards at the rigging, watching seagulls fly past.

Financed by Norwegian entrepreneur Sigurd Aase and launched in 2012, the *Draken Harald Hårfagre* is named after the Norwegian word for dragon, *draken*, and King Harald Fairhair, who unified Norway into one kingdom in the ninth century. Boatbuilders, historians, craftsmen, and artists labored for two years in Haugesund, Norway, to craft the longboat, using traditional methods and materials as much as possible. Thanks to them, *Draken* is as close as we can get to a Norse time machine.

After introducing myself to the man taking tickets, I found out what modern-day Vikings do when it's blistering hot: "Let's go below deck to find some air-conditioning," said David Short, the crew member who was tasked with showing me around the boat. Grateful for the offer but feeling unworthy of my Norse ancestry, I followed him down a couple of steps into a cramped space lined with two rows of bunks. The accommodations were far from luxurious, but the cool air blowing out of a small air conditioner felt heavenly. "The original Viking ships didn't have space like this under their decks, let alone air conditioning, of course, but we've made a few modifications to accommodate our crew," explained David. "The Norse would have lived and slept on the deck no matter what the weather, though they might well have constructed simple shelters to provide at least some protection from the elements."

In talking with David I learned that a blend of old and new technologies is a theme of the entire boat. When history enthusiasts first tried to re-create a Viking vessel, they followed models that included the Oseberg and Gokstad ships in the Oslo museum, only to find that their reconstructions weren't very seaworthy. In fact, several sank because it was difficult to guess exactly how they were constructed or sailed using only the archaeological evidence. In building the *Draken*, designers tried to balance historical accuracy with elements that would allow the boat to make trans-Atlantic voyages.

The result is a ship that measures 115 feet from stem to stern and 26 feet across, with oak used for the main body and Douglas fir for its 79-foot mast. Its square sail is made of silk, a sail that only kings could have afforded in the Viking era but which was chosen because it's lighter and easier to handle than a traditional woolen sail. Twenty-five pairs of oars provide backup for when the winds don't cooperate. Richly detailed carvings adorn the *Draken*'s sleek lines, including the dragon head, coiled tail, and two ravens that perch near the back of the ship, an homage to the birds that Odin sent out each day to gather information for him.

"The thing is, we really don't know much about how Viking boats were either built or sailed, so we have to make a lot of educated guesses," explained David. "And it's important to keep in mind that while they're historical artifacts to us, when they were first built these longboats were revolutionary, state-of-the-art vessels. You might think of them as the equivalent of spaceships taking off into the unknown. The Vikings were the astronauts of their time."

I savored the image of Vikings in spacesuits swinging broadswords while floating against a backdrop of stars, then listened as David told me about his own path to becoming a Norse sailor. As a college student he'd traveled from his native England to Oslo, where visits to the Viking ships, the polar explorer ship *Fram,* and Thor Heyerdahl's *Kon-Tiki* ignited a fascination for Norwegian sailing traditions. Though he hadn't spent much time on boats before, he learned to sail and started volunteering on historic replicas, eventually working his way up to the position of watch leader on the *Draken.*

"My passion is the history of sailing," he said. "I have about a decade of experience on Viking ships, which I guess makes me among the most experienced longboat sailors in the world. It's a wonderful challenge to try to figure out how to sail them. Even with modern gear and the chance to warm up below deck when you're off duty, it's hard, especially in the North Atlantic, where the conditions can be brutal. Your body almost goes into shock from the rain, wind, and cold. It gives you an appreciation for what the Vikings endured. They were so much tougher than we are. Even today, you know when you sail out of a harbor that whatever comes, you're going to have to deal with it on your own. I was on board once when the mast snapped in half, for example. It was a miracle that no one was injured or killed."

Another strong experience was the first time the *Draken* was taken out in rough water on a trip between the Shetland and Faroe Islands. A motorboat accompanied the longboat in case it ran into trouble, but the *Draken* had a mind of its own and went so fast that it left the other boat far behind. "The speed-to-weight ratio of a longboat is nearly equivalent to that of a modern racing yacht," explained David. "It's very stable and buoyant, like a leaf on the water, and it flexes as it sails, so much that rivets sometimes pop out from its sides."

His description made me remember that the Vikings considered their boats to be almost alive. It's no wonder they loved them so much they wanted to be buried with them. Hearing David's obvious affection for this boat showed that modern sailors can still fall under the spell of these amazing vessels.

Emerging from the cool cabin back into the heat again, I introduced myself to other crew members. The boat carries a crew of about thirty, aided by volunteers who sign up for weeklong stints. One man told me he'd caught the Viking bug as a child when his parents gave him a toy longboat. Another volunteer had considerable experience on eighteenth-century ships and was eager to learn how to sail an even older style of vessel.

I especially enjoyed visiting with a fellow writer, a woman who was working on a historical novel set during the Viking Age. "I've done a lot of book research, but there's no substitute for actually being here," she told me. "When I heard that the *Draken* was coming to our area, I knew I could learn more by being on it for an hour than I could by doing months of research in a library. I first came as a visitor, and when the crew saw how fascinated I was, they asked me to volunteer. They said it's the experience of a lifetime."

I told her about my own book project, and we compared notes about our experiences. Once you start digging into Viking history, we agreed, it can take years before you come up for air again.

During the rest of the day, I watched with interest as a steady stream of visitors boarded the *Draken*. Some had come because they had Scandinavian ancestry, but many more were there because they loved the TV shows *Vikings* and *Game of Thrones* and wanted to learn about the history behind the legends and stories. Our conversations made me realize that in the modern world, Vikings often sail into our lives through films, novels, and games, which I guess is appropriate, given how much the Norse loved stories and gaming.

Thinking about those conversations, I recalled David Short's response when I asked him which nationalities are most excited to tour the *Draken* on its journeys to ports of call throughout Europe and the United States. "Oh, it's the Americans who are most excited, by far," he'd said. "It's a very American thing to be obsessed with history—maybe it's because you're a land of immigrants, and you have so little history of your own. If you go to other parts of the world, everyone is descended from the same people, so you don't really think that much about your ancestors. But in America, most people come from a mix of ethnicities and think it's fun to explore them. If they're Italian, they imagine they're Romans. It's a little silly, really."

I nodded, choosing not to tell him about my own imaginary adventures with the Vikings. His comments certainly fit with what I'd heard from our friends in Bergen, the ones who told me that they knew few Norwegians who'd taken a DNA test. "We already know who we are," they'd said.

Perhaps we Americans *don't* know who we are, and that's why millions of us trace our genealogies and test our DNA. We're searching for roots and a story that can tie together the disparate parts of our lives and help us form our identities. That would help explain why all these people had ventured out on a sweltering day to tour a Norse ship, even if they have no ties to Scandinavia and their only connection to the Vikings is a TV series or superhero movie.

I spoke to a lost-looking teenager wearing a T-shirt bearing the name of a heavy metal band, a young man who'd come onto the boat alone. "I'm not sure why I'm here," he said in answer to my question. "I heard about the boat and something pulled me here."

Watch out, I felt like telling him. That's how it starts.

Worn out by the heat, I found a quiet spot at the back of the *Draken*, near one of the carved ravens that perched on either side of the vessel. I wondered how many visitors knew the birds weren't just decorations but Odin's scouts. I could feel the rocking of the boat and welcomed a slight breeze that brought a hint of coolness. I thought of what it would be like to sail on this boat, to cancel my flight back to Iowa and instead join the crew as it continued its journey southward. Of course they weren't *really* Vikings, just as the reenactors in Moorhead weren't really Norse. But they clearly had some of the Viking spirit, and I felt an undeniable kinship with them.

I recalled David Short's words about what set the Vikings apart from their contemporaries. "I think a small percentage of people in every generation have an itch to see what's over the next hill," he said. "It's like a recessive gene that gets passed from generation to generation. That's what the Vikings had, and I have it too."

Sitting there with one of Odin's ravens looking over my shoulder, I realized that his comment crystalized much of what I'd learned from my search for my spiritual and ancestral roots. That recessive gene for travel and adventure gave me a clue to understanding my own story. Though the Vikings had it in spades, as did my immigrant ancestors who'd left everything behind for a new life in America, through the following generations it had gone largely dormant. My parents and grandparents, wonderful people though they were, viewed travel with the deepest suspicion. Even a trip to a seemingly friendly state like Wisconsin or Minnesota held multiple risks—uncomfortable beds, unfamiliar roads, the prospect of getting lost. Best just to stay home, both physically and spiritually.

For whatever reason, however, I inherited the explorer's gene. It helps explain why I've long felt like a chick that had been put into the wrong nest at birth. Maybe that gene was why I've followed such a nomadic path, never feeling as alive as when I'm on the move, and why I'm endlessly curious about spiritual matters. If I'd been born during the Viking Age, I'd probably have been one of those who went *a-viking*. I'd have brought back a Buddha from my trip to Asia, too, like the one that turned up in the Swedish archaeological dig. In Ireland I'd have struck up a friendship with the monks (I hope I wouldn't have stolen from them as well, but I probably would have, given the peer pressure). In Constantinople I hope I wouldn't have scratched graffiti into the balcony railing but instead peered down in curiosity at the grandeur of the Christian liturgy unfolding below.

By now I'd traveled thousands of miles, from Minnesota and Philadelphia to England, Newfoundland, and Norway. I'd revisited the ethnic traditions of the small town where I grew up and journeyed through history courtesy of the Norse sagas. I'd lived as a Norse woman for a weekend (well, sort of) and learned how to consult the Norse runes when I needed guidance. I was especially grateful to the two people who'd been my guides through much of my quest: Gudrid the Far Traveler and Leif Eriksson the Lucky. On the bare bones of their narratives I'd constructed my own personal myth that tied me to them and to a much larger story.

I looked at my watch and realized it was time to go. The boat was filling with people, and my spot was no longer quiet. I rubbed my hand on the raven's beak, wishing him safe voyages, then made my way to the plank that led to the dock. The woman I'd met earlier, the one working on a historical novel, was taking tickets and greeted me as I approached.

"I envy you," I said. "You're going to have a great week."

She smiled, nodding. "Good luck on your own writing project," she said. "We're both traveling with the Vikings."

Then a voice spoke, and we turned to see a man exiting the boat behind me. Tall, with a shock of white hair and piercing blue eyes, he had a commanding air about him despite a substantial paunch and slightly disheveled clothes. "It's a good thing to delve into the past," he said, looking at me with an intensity that was weird, in the fullest Norse sense of that word. I suddenly had the feeling that he was more than just another tourist.

His gaze grew even more intense as he asked me a question, his voice deep and resonant: "Tell me, are your ancestors talking to you yet?"

I felt the hair rise up on my arms. "Why, yes, I guess they are," I said, stammering a bit, taken aback by his directness.

He nodded, then without another word turned and walked away down the dock, limping a little. I watched him until he disappeared around a corner, realizing that he bore an unmistakable resemblance to Odin, who often traveled in disguise. A down-on-his-luck, slow-moving Odin, but the father of the Norse pantheon nevertheless. I shook my head, the thought both intriguing and unsettling, and then stepped off the boat and onto the dock, curious about where both of us were headed next.

A Norse Cheat Sheet

Norse Terms and Concepts

Norns: the supernatural beings who decide the fate of every human

Völva: a staff-carrying woman who during the Viking Age served as a spiritual leader and healer

Wyrd: fate or destiny; the origin of the word *weird*

Web of Wyrd: the energetic matrix that connects everything in the past and present, as well as future potential events

Öorlog: an individual's destiny that is formed by DNA, ancestral karma, and inherited conditions, plus the accumulation of our actions, words, and intentions in our present lifetimes

Yggdrasil: The huge tree that connects the nine worlds of the Norse cosmos

An Approximate Guide to Norwegian and Old Norse Pronunciation

Å: "o" as in *more*

Æ: "a" as in *sad*

Ø (in Norwegian) and Ö (in Old Norse): "i" as in *girl*

Acknowledgments

The Web of Wyrd has connected me with many wonderful people during the writing of this book. In Newfoundland, Clayton Colbourne, Denecka Burden, Andre Myers, and Dale Wells introduced me to Norse history at L'Anse aux Meadows and Norstead. Jerry Paulson of the Norwegian American Genealogical Center and Midge Kjome of the Decorah Genealogy Association taught me about genealogy and helped me trace the lives of Hans and Sila. Laurann Gilbertson at Vesterheim Norwegian-American Museum and Heidi Sherman at the University of Wisconsin–Green Bay provided valuable research assistance. Deirdre McCloskey, Loren Horton, and Jeff Klahn were early readers of the manuscript and offered helpful suggestions. *Tusen takk* to all of you.

My quest for my roots was greatly enhanced by my friendship with Inta Tove Gundersen Taranrød. Many thanks to her and her husband Helge for hosting my family and me so generously and for their insights into Norwegian culture and history.

I'm grateful to Kari Tauring for teaching me about the Völva Stav path and inviting me to go along with her to the Midwest Viking Festival. Thanks to David Short for teaching me about Viking ships, to Claudia McGehee for her beautiful map and illustrations, and to Virginia Houser for her enthusiasm for all my writing projects and for accompanying me on a very warm and humid research trip to Philadelphia.

I'm grateful to my agent, Greg Daniel, and editor, Jessica Miller Kelley, for their support, encouragement, and skillful guidance.

Writing this book has made me more aware than ever before of the importance of family. I'm grateful to the Erickson,

Espeseth, Hill, and Bolson families, who kept ties alive through multiple generations, and to my stepson Erik Sessions and his family, who have put down their own deep roots in our mutual hometown of Decorah, Iowa. I remember with great fondness my friend Mark Jones, who taught me that families can be made by love as well as blood. I appreciate my sister Julie Fahlin's support for this project, including her good humor on our trip to Norway. My sterling sons Owen and Carl Sessions indulged my enthusiasms, asked good questions, and gave me valuable feedback on my manuscript. And Bob Sessions is my photographer, traveling companion, editor, and ever-marvelous husband. Thank you, once again and always.

After completing this manuscript, I had one more task: I traveled to the grave of Hans and Sila and sprinkled on it the dirt I'd brought back from Norway, blending the poor soil of Norway with the rich loam of Iowa. To Hans and Sila, and to all my ancestors, I dedicate this book with gratitude and admiration.

Notes

24 *"If you built a time machine and traveled"*: Christine Kenneally, *The Invisible History of the Human Race: How DNA and History Shape Our Identities and Our Futures* (New York: Viking Press, 2014), 219.

35 *"I have never seen more perfect"*: Neil Oliver, *The Vikings* (New York: Pegasus Books, 2014), 109–10.

46 *"The line separating good and evil"*: Aleksandr I. Solzhenitsyn, *The Gulag Archipelago*, vol. 2, trans. Thomas P. Whitney (New York: Harper Perennial Modern Classics, 2007), 615.

49 The information about Leif Eriksson and family is adapted from *The Vinland Sagas*, trans. Keneva Kunz (London: Penguin Classics, 2008), 3–50.

80 *"One gets the impression from"*: Birgitta Linderoth Wallace, *Westward Vikings: The Saga of L'Anse aux Meadows* (St. John's, NL: Historic Sites Association of Newfoundland and Labrador, 2012), 78.

90 *"Tolkien, who could speak"*: from Guy Davenport's introduction to Burton Raffel's *Pure Pagan: Seven Centuries of Greek Poems and Fragments* (New York: The Modern Library, 2005), 1.

92 *"Of every living creature they offer"*: H.R. Ellis Davidson, *Myths and Symbols in Pagan Europe: Early Scandinavian and Celtic Religions* (Syracuse, NY: Syracuse University Press, 1988), 59.

95 *"Fate occupied roughly the same"*: Daniel McCoy, *The Viking Spirit: An Introduction to Norse Mythology and Religion* (CreateSpace Independent Publishing Platform, 2016), 73.

106 *"People love it because"*: Harry Brumpton, "Top 10 Re-enactments for History Lovers," *Courier-Mail*, Brisbane, Queensland, Australia, July 7, 2012.

127 *"The high point of the rune-stone story"*: The description of the Kensington Rune Stone pageant is adapted from David M. Krueger, *Myths of the Rune Stone: Viking Martyrs and the*

Birthplace of America (Minneapolis: University of Minnesota Press, 2015), 1–4.

127 *"secret calendrical [sic] data"*: Erik Wahlgren, *The Vikings and America* (New York: Thames and Hudson, 1986), 132.

136 *"A myth, therefore, is true"*: Karen Armstrong, *A Short History of Myth* (Edinburgh, UK: Canongate, 2005), 10.

137 *"The . . . runecaster uses the [runes]"*: Paul Rhys Mountfort, *Nordic Runes: Understanding, Casting, and Interpreting the Ancient Viking Oracle* (Rochester, VT: Destiny Books, 2003), 141.

145 *"I in no way wish"*: quoted in Odd S. Lovoll, *The Promise of America: A History of the Norwegian-American People* (Minneapolis: University of Minnesota Press, 1984), 17.

166 *"We have it good"*: quoted in Odd S. Lovoll, *The Promise of America: A History of the Norwegian-American People* (Minneapolis: University of Minnesota Press, 1984), 68.

170 *"Naming a newborn child after"*: Daniel McCoy, *The Viking Spirit: An Introduction to Norse Mythology and Religion* (CreateSpace Independent Publishing Platform, 2016), 90.

171 *"in Norwegian"*: Lovoll, *The Promise of America*, 327.

187 *"The Norns did both"*: Mindy MacLeod and Bernard Mees, *Runic Amulets and Magic Objects* (Woodbridge, UK: Boydell Press, 2006), 39.

201 *"A hero is defined not by"*: Tom Shippey, *Laughing Shall I Die: Lives and Deaths of the Great Vikings* (London: Reaktion Books, 2018), 37.